LIFE SKILLS WORKBOOK FOR TEENS WITH AUTISM AND SPECIAL NEEDS

Susan Jules

© **Copyright 2020 - All rights reserved.**

It is not legal to reproduce, duplicate, or transmit any part of this document in either electronic means or in printed format. Recording of this publication is strictly prohibited and any storage of this document is not allowed unless with written permission from the publisher except for the use of brief quotations in a book review

Get the Letter of Intent FOR FREE.

Sign up for the no-spam newsletter, and get the LETTER OF INTENT for free.

Details can be found at the end of the book.

The author and publisher have provided this e-book to you for your personal use only. You may not make this e-book publicly available in any way. Copyright infringement is against the law. If you believe the copy of this e-book you are reading infringes on the author's copyright, please notify us at diffnotless.com/piracy

Table of Contents

Chapter 1 1

Introduction 1

    A. Teenagers, Autism Spectrum Disorder, and Special Needs 1

    B. Autism Spectrum Disorder 2

    C. Common Symptoms of Autism Spectrum Disorder 4

    D. Teens with Special Needs 9

    E. Neurotypical Teens and Their Challenges 15

Chapter 2 22

Social Skills 22

    A. Importance of Social Activities for Teens with Autism 23

    B. Augmenting Social Skills for Teens with Autism Spectrum Disorder and Special Needs 23

    C. Teaching Social Skills 25

    D. Existing Social Groups 27

    E. Encouraging Your Teen to Be Open and Honest About their Disorder 30

    F. Encouraging Your Teen to Ask for Home Visits from Friends... 30

    G. Engaging Activities for Teenagers with Autism 30

Chapter 3 32

v

Social Skills Continued	32
A. Individual Activities for Adolescents	32
B. Group activities for Adolescents	42

Chapter 4 53

Social Skills—Activities to Develop Sensory Skills 53

A. Staring Contest	53
B. Spot the Difference	55
C. Emotion Simulations	57
D. Matching Game	59
E. Watching TV Programs	61

Chapter 5 64

Social Skills Continued 64

A. Games That Involve Taking Turns	64
B. Creative Activities for Teenagers with Autism	67
C. Picking the Right Activities	73

Chapter 6 76

Friendship Skills 76

A. Why Friendships Are Important For Teenagers	78
B. Results of the Study on Autism and Friendship Skills	79
C. Helping Your Child with Autism Spectrum Disorder	80

Chapter 7 86

Friendship Skills—Developing Friendships 86

	A.	Initiate and Reciprocate 86
	B.	Get Involved 89
	C.	Encourage Age-Appropriate Activities When Possible 92
	D.	Blend In 94
	E.	Practice Good Hygiene.. 96
	F.	Know What's Trending.. 98

Chapter 8 101

Friendship Skills 101

	A.	Autism Spectrum Disorder and Bullying 101
	B.	Signs That a Teenager with Autism Is Being Bullied 103
	C.	Speaking to Teenagers with Autism About Bullying 105
	D.	Collaborating with Schools on Bullying 106
	E.	Supporting Teenagers with Autism at Home 107
	F.	When Teenagers with Autism Are Bullying Others 108
	G.	Strategies for Handling Bullying.. 109

Chapter 9 115

Friendship Skills—Peer Pressure and Peer Influence on Teenagers with Autism 115

	A.	Finding a Balance for Peer Pressure and Peer Influence 116
	B.	Helping Your Child Manage Peer Pressure and Peer Influence 118
	C.	Encourage a Wide Social Network 123
	D.	When You're Concerned about Peer Pressure and Peer Influence 124

	E.	When to Be Concerned about Peer Influence and Peer Pressure 125
	F.	Children at Risk of Negative Peer Pressure and Influence 126

Chapter 10 127

Life Skills 127

	A.	What Are Life Skills? 128
	B.	Determining Which Life Skills to Teach 129
	C.	Strategies for Teaching Life Skills 130

Chapter 11 137

Life Skills—Safety Awareness 137

	A.	In the Community 138
	B.	Public Transportation 140
	C.	Shopping in the Community 142
	D.	Law Enforcement 144
	E.	Internet Safety 147
	F.	Money Management 148
	G.	Sexual Awareness and Autism Spectrum Disorder 149

Chapter 12 153

Life Skills—Self-Determination/Advocacy 153

	A.	What Is Self-Advocacy? 153
	B.	How Can You Help Teenagers with Autism Spectrum Disorder Learn to Self-Advocate? 154
	C.	Educate the Teen on the Difference between Needs and Preferences 156

D.	Have Teens Write a Note to Their Teachers	158
E.	Include the Child in Individualized Education Program Meetings	159
F.	Encourage the Teen to Share Information with the Right People	161

Chapter 13 163

Life Skills—The Seven Essential Life Skills for Success in Teenagers with Autism 163

A.	Executive Functioning Skills	163
B.	Practical Living Skills	163
C.	Personal Care	164
D.	Job Skills	165
E.	Personal Safety	165
F.	People Skills	165

Chapter 14 168

Life Skills—Ten Ways to Build Your Teen's Independence 168

A.	Strengthen Communication	168
C.	Teach Your Child to Ask for a Break	169
D.	Work on Household Chores	170
G.	Build Leisure Skills	172
H.	Teach Self-Care during Adolescence	173
I.	Work on Vocational Skills	174

Chapter 15 176

Life Skills—Personal Finance 176

	A.	Tips to Help with Money Management through Daily Activities 177
	B.	Transportation 179
	C.	Public Transport Tips that are Autism Friendly 180

Chapter 16 183

Life Skills—Teaching Adolescents with Autism to Drive 183

	D.	Resources for Families 185

Chapter 17 187

Life Skills—Career Path and Employment 187

	A.	Plan at a Young Age 187
	B.	Capabilities-based Job Options 188
	C.	Hard Skills and Soft Skills 189
	D.	Parent Involvement at Every Level 189
	E.	Considering College as an Option 190

Chapter 18 193

Life Skills—Leisure/Recreation 193

	A.	Why is Developing Leisure Skills Important? 193
	B.	Qualities that Make Leisure Materials and Activities More Effective 194
	C.	How Can I Keep My Child Engaged After School? 197
	E.	Self-Care Skills 202

Chapter 1

Introduction

A. Teenagers, Autism Spectrum Disorder, and Special Needs

Life becomes increasingly challenging for parents once their wards enter their teenage years. Such challenges do get on the nerves of every parent; however, they are necessary for the formation and eventual exploration of the child's liberty and independence. It is imperative for us to comprehend the circumstance and problems which tweens and teens face if we are to better understand adolescents on the spectrum or those with special needs. This is because a lot of the challenges grown-ups encounter with adolescents on the spectrum or who have special needs are typically founded upon the fact that they are teens.

It is never easy to manage a teen, not to mention handling one with autism spectrum disorder (ASD) or other forms of special needs. The process of learning deepens and might become elusive if the parent or caregiver doesn't remain persistent. But with each learning curve comes the reality of results; it wouldn't take long before the parent becomes confident enough to allow the child to explore their independence. This feeling and action can be scary, but is necessary for both parents and teens.

Teenage social relationships can be problematic, particularly for older children and teenagers with ASD. Approaches such as role-play, video modeling, social stories, prompt cards, and hobby groups can help teenagers exercise the social skills they need for constructive social living.

For the teenage child with ASD, there are stacks of positive aspects to having hale and hearty relationships with peers. They can improve the self-esteem of the child and their sense of belonging. In addition, friendships and social relationships give the child the know-how for managing emotions, reacting to the feelings of others, as well as improving their ability in negotiation, cooperation, and solving problems.

However, teenage social relationships are also packed with social guidelines that usually go unsaid and that the child might find perplexing. The youngster would have to learn these guidelines alongside other elementary social skills such as knowing what is and isn't proper to say to others.

It doesn't matter if the child prefers to be on their own or has one or many friends; a good number of social skills will help them know how to act in altered social circumstances, from chatting with a shopping mall aide to being part of family assemblies or enjoying themselves at teenage parties.

B. Autism Spectrum Disorder

Autism spectrum disorder is a name that is used to refer to wide-ranging neurodevelopmental disorders that can be witnessed through particular deeds, communication practices, and panaches of social interactions. Autism is also referred to as a *spectrum disorder;* this is due to the outward signs of the disorder ranging on a spectrum from them not being very obvious (mild) to them being very conspicuous (severe) as equated with what most people would call the *social norm* (neurotypical).

Research from recent editions of the Diagnostic and Statistical Manual of Mental Disorders (DSM-5) show that physicians make a diagnosis of ASD by pinpointing more than a few fundamental signs. However, the signs of ASD arguably vary extensively from one individual to another. These signs are also notorious for changing, as the person grows older. This implies that ASD signs experienced in childhood may completely differ from those the patient may experience in adolescence or teenage years.

Here are some facts about ASD:

- Autism spectrum disorder is a disorder that is not fully understood by medical professionals; it affects certain parts of the brain; it is not a disease in itself; it isn't transmissible; and there is no cure.
- One out of every 150 people is believed to have ASD.
- Autism Spectrum Disorder is seven times more common in boys compared to girls.
- It is common for teens with ASD to want to fit in, and they typically do not opt to act differently from other teens.

- Some of their unusual actions might stem from ignorance of the nature of inappropriateness of their actions toward others.

- Teens with ASD are unique; they are as distinct from each other as you and I are.

Teens with ASD do have a number of strengths:

- Some can be extremely meticulous, which is an excellent trait for developing expertise in certain fields, such as computers, gaming, science, or statistics.

- A lot of ASD teens are very good at memorizing.

- Their attention to detail can be exceptionally high.

- A lot are defenseless when it comes to being helped and therefore can be eager to learn.

- They rarely meddle in lies.

C. Common Symptoms of Autism Spectrum Disorder

Teens on the spectrum face challenges of adolescence as well as added challenges due to symptoms brought about by their condition. An appraisal of the symptoms of ASD can help one understand the importance of the numerous investigations carried out to expose the core symptoms of these disorders and also understand how challenging the diagnosis can be. A known teen on the spectrum may not display any individual symptom. Likewise, the ruthlessness of symptoms may differ extensively among teens.

A lot of the social complications of teens on the spectrum can be attributed to the misleading of teachers into assuming that these teens know more than they do, have reached an impasse in expressing themselves to others, and have deficits in appreciating others and coping with anxiety-provoking circumstances. Below are a few symptoms, amongst which are those that have a higher need to be handled and those that appear less dominant to social adjustment.

Disingenuous aspects of communication.
Typically, students on the spectrum appear reasonably verbal; however, quite a few features of ASDs do cover deficits, crafting a false impression of age-appropriate or progressive skills. Furthermore, the detail-oriented, overly ceremonial style of expression of these teens on the spectrum may give the impression that they appreciate things more than they do. These teens are sometimes labeled as having nonverbal learning disabilities. However, on standardized IQ tests, their scores are usually comparable in verbal and nonverbal areas to those of their neurotypical peers.

In contrast, they show comparatively poor performance on verbal skills such as social judgment and appreciation of social contracts. They tend to have good memorization skills and a good grasp of factual material, leading various teachers to consider them quite intelligent in a wide-ranging sense. However, this can be very deceptive. Higher hopes that arise from this false impression can be demanding for both teachers and teens.

Hiccups in expression and communication.

We communicate not only with words but through our gestures and facial expressions too as we speak. We also sometimes hide our true intent in a conversation so as not to make our listeners uncomfortable. Tweens and teens on the spectrum miss many of these conversational nuances.

Nonverbal aspects of communication.

Teens on the spectrum may be unsuccessful in using nonverbal aspects of communication. They display very minimal body language, uphold too little or too much social distance from their listener, and have flat or infrequent voice pitch disparity and inflection. Perhaps the most stigmatizing aspect is social distance. This is because it breeds uneasiness in listeners. This is fairly easy to correct, as the rule of good manners is to stay about an arm's length from your listener while refraining from measuring it with your arms.

Additionally, teens on the spectrum do not usually display their agony using voice tone or other nonverbal cues, such that a circumstance can escalate extensively before others are sentient of their difficulties. It is established that teaching teens on the spectrum how to diagnose their anxiety helps them lessen their anxiety and avert eventual meltdowns.

Social aspects of communication.

Students on the spectrum often miss the more formal parts of conversations. They also often miss the point of the short "How are you?" conversation often going on for too long. They can be quite direct in their communications, which others often misconstrue as insolence.

Adolescents on the spectrum are well known for having poor eye contact during social conversations. Extensive research has revealed that lower-functioning individuals on the spectrum have strange patterns of visually glancing over their environment. Neurotypical males have shoddier eye contact in conversations than neurotypical females do. Nonetheless, high-functioning teens on the spectrum, being mostly males, typically do not display conspicuous variances from other males in social eye contact during conversations. Furthermore, teaching teen boys to give eye contact with other teen boys will most probably make the other teen boys feel uncomfortable.

Cognitive inflexibility.

A lot of teens on the spectrum prefer everything to be the same and everything to be in what they view as the right place. They can get very distraught and are sure to point it out if something is done in what they consider "the wrong way," especially as it has to do with their focal interest, if they have one. For some teens on the spectrum, this is articulated in little dissimilarity in the clothing they wear. Even though these teens are poor at setting up routines for effective self-organization, they may strictly follow their routine, in the same way, every day. Thus, any changes in school routines may be especially puzzling for them.

They profit immensely by being cautioned in advance and specifically how things in their routines are about to change and will need much tailored assistance on managing the change. On the other hand, many teens on the spectrum may have had a barely limited range of interests as children but are now ready to expand their interests. These adolescents are able to widen their range as long as their anxiety doesn't get in the way.

Humor production.

Research has pointed out that those telling jokes have a tendency to harm the development of friendship. A lot of teens on the spectrum have difficulty with both appreciating the humor of others and conveying their jokes. Their humor leans toward being more symptomatic of much younger children, as research indicates that only 16 percent of adults on the spectrum could tell jokes that were age-appropriate for teens and adults. When asked to pick funny punch lines for jokes in one study, teens on the spectrum were disposed to pick punch lines that were unrelated to the content of jokes or picked straightforward endings that were not humorous at all.

For these reasons, joke-telling tends to further stigmatize most teens on the spectrum and should be discouraged in most cases.

Conversational repair processes.

Teens on the spectrum are usually better at engaging in virtual or written conversations than verbal conversations. This is because they have time to process more fully what has been said in a written conversation, while the content of conversations is not as available after it has been said, and the listener is under pressure to respond more quickly than in a written conversation. Neurotypical teens have skills to ensure that they understand what has transpired, and they use these skills to "repair" the conversation to full comprehension. In contrast, teens on the spectrum may know they missed something but lack repair skills.

D. Teens with Special Needs

A lot of teens find it tough to uphold their self-image; however, teens with special needs, such as learning disabilities, are for the most part vulnerable. This is because they are cognizant of the fact that they have more learning troubles compared to their peers; this can breed feelings of shame, low self-esteem, worries about the future, and eventual failure.

As children with disabilities or special health care needs navigate their way from childhood to adulthood, they do encounter an array of difficulties. It is typical for physical and hormonal changes to take a toll on both the parent and the youngster. Furthermore, the teen might need help appreciating these changes to their body and where to apply appropriate behaviors. And as puberty sets in, the youngster will most likely have a lot of questions about sexuality. These subjects are usually tough for any parent to confront. It is possible that the parent would experience frustration when the child comes across an activity or milestone that other teenagers do with more ease. The child may find it challenging to date, ride, drive, or take certain steps that their peers take to display their independence.

It is noteworthy to say that all teens do find it hard to feel like they fit in, regardless of whether or not they have a disability or special health care need. It is therefore important for the parents to constantly remind themselves and their child that being a teenager has no one "right" way to go about it. Perhaps the child might do better by talking to a mentor or by spending time with peers that have a similar disability or special health care needs. Parents should simply give the child all the support and encouragement needed and do whatever is required to foster the child's independence, helping them take necessary steps that would lead to such paths.

Tweens and teens who struggle with ASD or other forms of special needs do desire to be a part of school life, even though they don't fully understand a lot about it and properly fit in. This is particularly unique to children within the spectrum. For them, growing up was filled with a lot of isolation from others on their part. And as they grew up, they triumphed over several barriers and are now making efforts to understand others. But due to the effect of their prolonged isolation, they have fallen behind in this understanding.

Here are some facts about teens with special needs:

- *Teens with learning disabilities have been known to possess average or higher IQ.* This diagnosis was done using a technique called an aptitude-achievement discrepancy method, which systematically compares the IQ scores of teens with learning disabilities with achievement test scores. The variations between those scores aid in determining the existence of learning disability. On the basis of the statistics obtained from this technique, it was determined that most students with special needs have an average or above average IQ to qualify for the diagnosis. Furthermore, teens with learning disabilities process information in certain unique ways compared to others.

- *Learning disabilities are typically differences in learning.* It is safe to say that every learner learns differently to some degree. While some learn better by reading, others may learn better by listening to a lecture. Still others learn best when the project is hands-on compared to when it involves complex thinking. Some learn best by reading, and others prefer to write. The list is limitless. One of the distinctive differences between students with learning disabilities and others is that the latter do not easily become accustomed to systematic classroom teaching as typically and as rapidly as their contemporaries do. This is because a lot of conventional classroom lessons are conveyed via lecture, reading of texts, and visual aids. Consequently, students who need tractability in instruction are left behind in the customary classroom.

- *Students with special needs learn at dissimilar rates.* Some students require supplementary time and familiarity with ideas for them to effectively grasp them. Students with special needs sometimes have to work with a distinct special education teacher in smaller groups; this gives room for them to have more time to learn than can be afforded in a conventional classroom setting. Students with learning disabilities require teaching that arranges for

- listening periods set aside for presented ideas in strides that are natural for them;

- pondering sessions for practicing presented ideas;

- occasions to work in clusters and added period for working individually if needed; and

- sufficient time for revision before moving on to other material.

- *Students with special needs learn best with diverse forms of materials.* Conventionally, teaching is done via lecture, the use of boards, overhead projectors, and handouts. These approaches, however, do not sufficiently meet the needs of all students, as research has shown that even students without disabilities do face difficulties in customary classrooms. Students with learning disabilities require a diversity of learning resources and tools, like hands-on projects, real-world-based experiments and experiences, and rational instances to connect newfangled knowledge to their previously assimilated ideas. In addition, they require evocative visual tools, multisensory learning gears, and malleable testing approaches that permit students to display what they've learned in ways that they are most comfortable with.

- *Students with learning disabilities often require differentiated instruction.* All students require diversity in their learning tools and added periods to effectively process information. Students with learning disabilities also require more responsiveness from teachers to the individual learning styles of the students. Special education refers to this as *differentiated instruction.* It has been clinically established that students with learning disabilities are more likely to require differentiated instruction in order to acclimatize to instructional materials enough to meet their needs.

- *Students with learning disabilities often experience bullying.* Like people with character flaws, bullies have grave behavioral complications that have little to do with the student and their disability. Bullies will take every chance they can find to pick on others; this makes it a serious problem. Parents, teachers, and schools need to enact and uphold laws in and around the learning environment that are aimed at protecting such vulnerable teens from such vicious attacks. Inasmuch as dealing with bullies (both physical and virtual) can help the child in developing certain levels of fortitude, it is best to help them get along with other teens and with their studies without getting severe emotional traumas from bullies.

Some common challenges that teens with ASD and special needs might exhibit:	
Ordinary conversation difficulties	- Forget to use greetings and closings, such as "hello" and "goodbye." - They may not understand slang (such as "get over it," "let's hang out," "put a sock in it," or "take a chill pill"). - They may not understand jokes or sarcasm and forget to ask when they don't understand. Sometimes, they don't understand what you are telling them. - Help them to feel comfortable asking questions when they don't understand. - They may have anxiety attacks, especially when they are under pressure. - They may not understand vague requests, such as "Come back later."
Body language difficulties	- They may either stand too close or too far away in conversation. - They may not understand hints.
Common social circumstance	- They may not have learned common sense

difficulties	about things you take for granted. For instance, they may not have enough common sense to avoid telling others when they break minor school rules.
	• They may make unintentionally rude comments, such as "you have bad breath."
	• They may benefit from gentle guidance about grooming and hygiene.

Many teens with ASD and other types of special needs work hard to learn suitable behaviors and how to deduce emotional meaning. Doing one's best to help would encourage them to continue learning about themselves and their classmates. After all, the students with ASD or other special needs are adolescents who desire to be respected as individuals and have fun.

E. Neurotypical Teens and Their Challenges

Students must be conversant with the following challenges if they are to be better adjusted, not only as teens but later as adults too. These challenges are well known to middle and high school teachers; however, they have been summarized in order to explain how each one affects the adolescent on the spectrum.

Becoming independent from parents.

Characteristically, adolescents become progressively more involved with and reliant on their peers. Studies have shown that they spend an average of 449 minutes per day with their peers, 248 minutes per day with parents at home, mostly watching TV together, and about 241 minutes per day alone. This is indicative of the fact that teens spend more time with their peers than with their parents or alone.

After taking a further look into all of the teens in the study, researchers saw that time spent with parents appeared to take away from the social lives of girls than from those of boys. This is because the teenage boys who spent more time with their parents did so at the cost of their alone time, while the teenage girls who spent more time with their parents did so at the cost of their time with peers. Consequently, while they become more reliant on peers, teens increasingly pull away from their parents and guardians.

Typically, the family affiliations of teens are stormier compared to those of other younger children; and in all likelihood, most of the conflicts revolve around the teens' struggle for greater self-sufficiency. This is notable as a typical teen averages about two conflicts every three days—and this conflict is with everyone. However, mothers are involved in more of these quarrels than fathers are; this may be because the former are generally more involved in child-rearing than the latter. More conflicts come with dire consequences, as the affection and helpfulness of these teens toward parents begin to face deterioration.

Even though some adolescents on the spectrum are more passive and childlike than their neurotypical peers, many become grumpier and act out more, particularly toward their parents. A lot of them turn out to be less keen to accept assistance and advice from their parents. The adolescents on the spectrum who are more outspoken in their tussle for independence may seem more challenging for parents. The problem with this quest for independence is that parents commonly recognize that adolescents aren't sufficiently prepared to manage much of what greater independence brings. They recognize more than their teens that teens on the spectrum could do with more tailored assistance with life challenges.

The declining relationships with their parents often indicate that teens seldom revert to them for help and guidance. More than ever before, it's helpful for these adolescents to have someone like a trusted teacher, peer, mentor, or guidance counselor to fill this void. They are probably going to welcome guidance and information if it comes from a trusted adult other than a parent.

Getting ready for a vocation or career.

It is common for vocational counselors to assess students for potential career choices by using two kinds of assessments, namely interests, and skills range assessment (fitting to careers where skills would be most useful) and people-type- based assessment (fitting based on preferences to the people with whom they like to associate).

A lot of young adults form many of their relationships at their job, and these relationships usually aid in improving job performance and job fulfillment. Relationship deficiencies of adolescents on the spectrum are as a consequence restrictive to their subsequent engagement, satisfaction, and performance on the job.

It is common for teens on the spectrum to somewhat grow out of some of their symptoms. So while they may have had a narrowly delimited range of interests as children, they are now ready to enlarge those. Students on the spectrum are capable of widening their range, provided they can keep a lid on their anxiety.

Regulating to the corporeal and psychosexual vagaries of puberty.
The bodies of teens tend to change alongside the social landscape around them, and usually, teens on the spectrum appear largely unprepared to meet such challenges of sexuality and romance. The more passive and naive tweens and teens on the spectrum may be the more oblivious they would be to these issues. They might fancy having a girlfriend or boyfriend, but it would most likely be characteristic of their social communications with peers in general. They usually are clueless about what it entails to have a romantic relationship. Boys on the spectrum may be particularly at risk due to allegations of harassment or stalking; girls, on the other hand, are particularly at risk of being ill-used or becoming targets.

Nurturing values and identity.
Studies that entailed the use of electronic pagers to prompt teens to report what they were up to and their emotional states all the way through the week stated that neurotypical teens spent an average of 25 percent of their waking hours in voluntary aloneness. Furthermore, the studies indicate that this solitude benefits them in

no small measure as those who spent between 30 and 40 percent of their waking hours alone had better grade point averages compared to their counterparts who spent either more or less time alone. Again, they were also appraised as better adjusted by their teachers and peers. Thus, adolescents on the spectrum may have the need for some amount of aloneness, mostly at home, in order to ponder their life challenges and changes as much as neurotypical teens do.

Forming actual relationships with peers.
Generally, high-functioning teens on the spectrum often desire to be more like the teens they see around them but lack the basic knowledge and the wherewithal to engage their peers effectively. This concept goes against early notions of individuals with autism who were characterized as having a prevailing yearning for aloneness. Further observation reveals that rather than choosing to be alone more than other teens do, a lot of these teens on the spectrum would prefer to mingle but are limited by their inability to form even peripheral friendships, and most can't or don't know how to become more intimate with the friends they already have.

Statistically, only 27 percent of students on the spectrum and 41 percent of students with other developmental disabilities reported having a best friend. This implies that students on the spectrum are mindful of being socially rejected, and a lot of them have limited knowledge of what a friend is. This is evident when for instance they admit to having one or two friends but can't recall their names. Furthermore, they may report having less satisfactory relationships and companionship with the friends they may have, along with more lonesomeness at school, compared with neurotypical peers. The unrelenting self-isolation of these teens makes inadequacies in the knowledge of peer propriety more evident as they get older. As adults, a lot of persons on the spectrum are deficient in community connections and friendships that neurotypical persons overlook.

However, neurotypical teens are capable of formulating relationships at numerous levels, which can be branded as their pack, their friends, and their very best friends. These youngsters look for others like themselves and then turn out to be more like those they associate with. Friends are comparable to each other on demographics, school-related approaches, and attitudes about teen culture such as drinking, smoking, drug use, dating, and involvement in parties, religious activities, dress sense, and grooming. All of these influences are centered in the *crowd*. The crowd is a distinctive class of fixed friendships that arises in teenage years, and each crowd is typically labeled by a name such as the Jocks, Burnouts, Computer Geeks, Rednecks, and so on.

In the crowd, teens form factions with four or so other teens. Unlike the factions in elementary school, mixed-gender factions occasionally form at this stage, and these clusters tend to be stable. While elementary school friendships deteriorate once the children are allotted to different classrooms at the beginning of each school year, middle and high school factions are unwavering across years and over the summer. This is because teens are able to travel to each other's houses and meet in different locations devoid of much parental involvement. In spite of the impact of the crowd in the process of defining teen identity, it has been mostly ignored by clinicians who are teaching teens on social skills, mostly disremembered by parents of teens on the spectrum, and mostly disregarded by the teens themselves, often at their social jeopardy.

In addition, psychological sharing is a vital part of a lot of teen friendships, particularly for girls, who tend to have a larger number of close friends compared to their male counterparts. Countless neurotypical boys possess poor-quality friendships that are competitive rather than intimate. As a result of this, the referral rate to social skills groups for neurotypical students is three times larger for boys than it is for girls.

Chapter 2

Social Skills

Social skills can be described as the ability of an individual to effectually interrelate and interconnect with others using their words, actions, and body language. As a result, how we acclimatize to social situations and interfaces is dependent on social skills. Typically, social skills are not always instinctive; however, they can be taught and learned over certain periods. So people with autism often require unambiguous instruction in order to thoroughly learn appropriate social skills and how to acclimatize to relations.

For parents or guardians of teens with autism or teens with special needs, it usually comes as no surprise that their wards tend to be less socially developed and active compared to their neurotypical counterparts. Furthermore, a study has indicated that neurotypical teens expect social rewards more intensely compared to their peers with ASD. It is clear that both internal and external forces may account for these differences; without a doubt, teens on the spectrum may find themselves contending with decreased social inspiration and ever-increasing sensory overload.

Teens with ASD are not commonly rewarded through social interactions as suggested by *the social motivation hypothesis*. This means that they may lack sufficient motivation to interact at all. On the other hand, *the sensory over-responsivity theory* suggests that teens with ASD interpret sensory cues at a greater rate of intensity; this propels them to avoid overwhelming social interactions.

A. Importance of Social Activities for Teens with Autism

Due to the difficulties teenagers with ASD have in communicating and socializing, coupled with a lack of some essential skills, they are extremely prone to social anxieties. To assist youth with autism to cultivate the required social skills and discover their identity, teachers and caregivers should engage them in social activities.

Social activities allow teenagers with autism to

- discover and nurture their interests.
- be buoyant and try new things.
- learn common social behavior.
- come across like-minded teens and spend some quality and learning time with them.
- learn new skills such as dancing, singing, sports and so on.

B. Augmenting Social Skills for Teens with Autism Spectrum Disorder and Special Needs

There are a number of things parents can do to help advance and enhance social skills in teens on the spectrum:

Introduce your teen to social groups.

Social groups and clubs aimed specifically toward youth with autism recommended by your teen's teacher or therapist may help the teen in learning to improve their social skills. Here, your teen will be able to come across others like them in a calm, well-ordered environment particularly tailored for young people with their condition.

Importance of social and recreational activities for teenagers with ASD

- Contrary to what people might think, teenagers with ASD, just like characteristically developing teenagers, are interested in recreational and social activities. They tend to relish as much pleasure from these activities.

- By attending such organized social and recreational activities with other young individuals, teenagers with ASD get the chance to explore distinct interests or things they're good at. Such adventures can aid them in building confidence, spotting, and learning useful skills for employment in later years.

- Teenagers with ASD have the opportunity to meet others who are interested in the same things when they attend social activities. This inspires feelings of inclusion and reduced feelings of aloneness or isolation. In addition, meeting people socially is a great way for teenagers with ASD to exercise social skills.

- Teenagers with ASD can benefit immensely from the organization and routine that structured social and recreational activities offer.

Where to begin with social activities

The ideal place to begin is to have a chat with your child about the activities or groups that they might be interested in. Start by exploring thoughts about

- undertakings that can be done by individuals.

- undertakings that could only be done by a group.

- novel groups of undertakings that can be pioneered by the teen.

- popular events for other teenagers with similar interests, strengths, and needs.

From time to time, there would be a need for you, an aide, or another support person to advocate for your child to ensure they are involved in the activities that they like, as everyone has a right to take part in activities and use amenities in the community.

C. Teaching Social Skills

Typically, social skills programs unambiguously teach tailored skills. Below is a chart that outlines various steps and ways to teach a range of social skills.

Teaching Steps	Teaching Methods
Introduce	Explanation, use of social tales, videos, rules.
Define	What it is. Use games, visual prompts.
Practice	Role-play, modeling (video and peer), comic strips
Generalize	Practice in nature, with multiple people, and in different places.

For instance, when trying to teach your child not to interrupt other people,

- Begin by introducing the skill.
    - Use a social story to clarify the act of interrupting.
- Then, define the skill.
    - Make a visual prompt of questions to ask yourself before speaking.
        - Is this an emergency?
        - Is the person already speaking to someone else?
        - How can I get the person's attention?

- Say, "Excuse me."
- Smile at the person, and wait.

- Next, practice using the skill.
  - Role-play not interrupting someone.
  - Practice diverse role-playing circumstances with peer models.
  - Watch a video showing a discussion where a person waits for their turn to speak.
- Finally, generalize the skill in numerous backgrounds.
  - Seek out conversations with a variety of people.

D. Existing Social Groups

It is recommended that when enlisting your child with ASD or any other special need into joining any group or activity that is already running in your community, it would be best to ensure that the choices match the teen's interests and strengths. Furthermore, the group must be ready to be flexible when it comes to meeting the teen's needs. You can have a conversation about existing groups and choose a few that will work for both your child and the group.

Below is a list of some popular community groups that you might have in schools or your community:

Groups	Examples
Scouts	- Boy scouts - Girl guides
Cocurricular groups	- The student council - Class representative group
Fan or creative writing groups	- Sci-fi clubs - Anime clubs - Comic hubs - Book clubs
Community-based or after-school clubs	- Drama - Math - Lego - Astronomy - Computer coding

	• Toastmasters
Outdoor activities	• Lawn bowling
	• Archery
	• Skating
	• Laser skirmish
Indoor activities	• Dance
	• Gymnastics
	• Indoor games like volleyball or swimming
Board activities	• Chess
	• Monopoly
	• Scrabble

In addition, there might also be organized social groups for teenagers with disabilities, as well as those with ASD. Cases in point are special sporting teams or campgrounds that teenagers can be enrolled in for a small fee.

E. Encouraging Your Teen to Be Open and Honest about Their Disorder

You can buoy up your teen to be open with others on the subject of their ASD status and to describe its traits to teachers and students alike. Additionally, you might wish to visit your teen's classrooms and help convey informational programs about ASD. It is generally anticipated that your kid's classmates coming to comprehend their situation could help discourage them from avoiding, mocking, or feeling ill at ease around them.

F. Encouraging Your Teen to Ask for Home Visits from Friends

It is also recommended that you buoy up your ASD teen to invite their friends over for games, movies, and parties; this is a perfect way to develop social skills in teens on the spectrum. Your teen may feel more at ease interrelating with peers on the territory: a place in which they feel relaxed, where their environment is well ordered and scrutinized, and they are not as likely to feel terrified or overwhelmed.

G. Engaging Activities for Teenagers with Autism

It has been statistically shown that classroom lectures aren't effective teaching methodologies for students with autism. Teenagers and young children with autism have a tendency to learn better when they are allowed to have practical experiences on the subject.

In the next chapter, there are some engaging activities to do with teenagers having autism; these activities are aimed at teaching and developing skills needed for a comfortable and confident social life.

Chapter 3

Social Skills Continued

A. Individual Activities for Adolescents

Typically, the rate at which kids with autism pick up social skills isn't as quickly or as easily as other children their age. Nevertheless, the parent can begin building the child's skills gradually. Here are the solo activities to do with teenagers with autism.

Reading simple, thought-provoking books

The idea	*Reading aids in the augmentation of cerebral functions and keeps the brain dynamic.*
	The parent can sit with their teen and encourage them to read educational, fiction, and scientific books that are easy to read and comprehend.
How it helps	• *develops language* • *improves learning and comprehension skills*
You will need	*A collection of interesting educational, scientific, and fiction books and novels.*
Type	*Indoor activity*

What to do:

- Begin by arranging and scheduling reading hours for your teen.

- Encourage the teen to read simple yet interesting books.

- You can go out of your way to research and recommend books that align with your set criteria. This can also be done with the teen; it would be fun.

Take note of the various responses of the teen at each stage and with each instruction.

Important notes:

_____

_____

_____

_____

_____

_____

_____

_____

_____

_____

Music therapy

The idea	Music is known to be therapeutic. Music therapy helps your adolescent with autism efficiently nurture language and speech abilities. Furthermore, music helps in the overall improvement of the teen's life and instills positive changes in behavior.
How it helps	- Relaxes the teenager - Reduces anxiety - Supports memory enhancement and communication
You will need	A collection of entertaining and enjoyable songs and themes
Type	Indoor activity

What to do:

- Begin by ensuring that the teen with autism listens to a number of interesting songs every day.

- You can also inspire the youngster to join music classes and sing simple songs.

- Buoy up the teen to participate in musical programs at school or college and sing in a choir.

- You can try introducing the teen to musical instruments. This is important, as the teen might enjoy playing an instrument more than singing.

> **Take note of the various responses of the teen at each stage and with each instruction.**

Important notes:
_____
_____
_____
_____
_____
_____
_____
_____
_____

Puzzles

The idea	*The idea behind a puzzle is about bringing different fragments together, adding up to something meaningful. Characteristically, teenagers with autism are visually skilled and enjoy working on puzzles. Most kids with autism have hyperfocus, which helps them in solving puzzles. Puzzles are also used to assist children with speech disabilities.*
How it helps	<ul><li>*Enhance cognitive abilities*</li><li>*Enhance speech and communication skills*</li><li>*Could also spark their imagination*</li></ul>
You will need	*Jigsaw puzzles of different levels—simple to complex*
Type	*Indoor activity*

What to do:

- You can begin by employing the use of puzzles in the day when you notice that the teen is becoming increasingly restless. Puzzles are excellent tools for engaging teenagers with autism.

- At first, you can begin with a simple puzzle before gradually increasing the level of difficulty.

- As the teen gets engrossed in the activity, you can try to get them to talk about what they are doing and thinking. This helps strengthen their communication skills.

- It is important to allow them to talk at their own pace, without you rushing them.

> **Take note of the various responses of the teen at each stage and with each instruction.**
>
> **Important notes:**
> _____
> _____
> _____
> _____
> _____
> _____
> _____
> _____
> _____
> _____

Computer Games

The idea	*Unlike what many people think, computer games are not all bad. The right games can teach your children a lot of things and help develop their skills. Research reveals that teenagers with autism can develop their social skills and problem-solving skills by playing computer games.* *Pick a computer game that matches your teen's IQ levels and skill level. Set aside half an hour every day in their schedule to play these games. Most teens with autism like a routine.*
How it helps	- *Improve social skills* - *Encourage them to use logic* - *Encourage imagination and creativity.*
You will need	- *Time management games* - *Role-play games* - *Storytelling games* - *Puzzles*
Type	*Indoor activity*

What to do:

- You can begin by allowing the teen to play a simple training game such as *Eric Goes to the Airport* or *Robbie the Robot Coaches*. These teach the kid about basic behavioral skills when in public.

- You can go further by introducing a role-play or a time management game.

- Massively Multiplayer Online (MMO) video games are an excellent idea for working on your teen's social skills. But be careful so that the teen doesn't get overly involved or is exposed to cyberbullying.

- Multiplayer games will also aid the teen in socializing with family and friends.

- You can help your kid even further by playing the games with them, engage them in conversations about the game while they play, and help them with tips on how to overcome challenging levels.

Take note of the various responses of the teen at each stage and with each instruction.

Important notes:

_____

_____

_____

_____

_____

_____

_____

_____

_____

Draw something app

The idea	*If your teenager likes technology, you can try getting them to use the app called Draw Something. This is a social drawing tool that lets the teen play with their friends and sends messages in the form of pictures they draw.*

How it helps	• *This app triggers imagination and creative communication skills.* • *It teaches the teen a creative way to express themselves.* • *It encourages hearing and wit in conversation and interaction.*
You will need	*A smartphone with the Draw Something app*
Type	*Indoor activity*

What to do:

- Begin by introducing the game to your teen. It is recommended that you use two phones to play the game with them first.

- Play the game with each other first and see how they respond. In all likelihood, your teen would like it.

- Once the kid is comfortable with it, you can teach them how to play the game with other online players.

> Take note of the various responses of the teen at each stage and with each instruction.

Important notes:

_____

_____

_____

_____

_____

_____

_____

_____

_____

B. Group activities for Adolescents.

One of the most essential parts of social skill development is interaction. Participating in team activities and events as much as possible is very important if you want to help your teen with autism with their social life. With that said, you should ensure that you do not push them into something they are not comfortable with. The idea is to ease them into society one step at a time.

Dancing

The idea	*Dancing is fun and will often promote happiness and mental freshness in kids with ASD. Dance is also a social activity that they may have to learn about to have fruitful romantic relationships in the future.*
How it helps	• *Increases social interaction skills* • *Boosts overall confidence*
You will need	• *Music* • *A place to dance*
Type	*Indoor and outdoor activity*

What to do:

- Begin by accessing a few dance videos online and showing them to your teen to introduce the concept.
- You can demonstrate to the teen how to dance; this is important as one of the best ways to teach something is through modeling that behavior. Better, dance with them.
- Ensure that you exhibit positive behavior and emotions when you dance; this will inspire the teen to try it.
- Make sure no one pulls them onto the dance floor. Allow them to come and join you themselves when they are ready.

- You can also schedule visits to events where people dance and have fun.

- You could also invite a few of your teen's friends for a dance party. Make sure your teen consents to this decision.

- It is common for the teen to dance as well if their friends dance.

Camping expedition

The idea	*In the event that your teenager already has a few social skills developed and can get along fairly well with different people in the group, camping would be a great idea to explore. Camping with friends and strangers can help in developing social skills and learning new life skills.*
How it helps	• *Cultivates social skills* • *Improves life skills*
You will need	• *Camping materials* • *Bags* • *Tents*
Type	*Outdoor activity*

What to do:

- Begin by taking your teen on a camping trip with the family. This will help them experience the event among people they are comfortable with first.

- Subsequently, plan a camping trip with a few friends that your teen is familiar with coupled with a few persons that they do not know. This concept will help the teen learn how to get along with people they meet for the first time.
- Once the teen gets the basic idea of what camping is about, you can encourage them to go on camping tours on their own, with their friends or group members.

> **Take note of the various responses of the teen at each stage and with each instruction.**
>
> **Important notes:**
> _____
> _____
> _____
> _____
> _____
> _____
> _____
> _____
> _____
> _____

Playing tennis

The idea	Tennis is an exceptional game for fitness of the body and mind. The game lets your teenager become bodily stronger while teaching them to strive sportively with other players.
How it helps	• Cultivates rule-keeping abilities • Improves overall physical health • Triggers and improves healthy competition
You will need	• Tennis racquets • Tennis balls • Tennis court
Type	Outdoor activity

hat to do:

- Begin by introducing the game to your teen with autism; you can do this by showing them a few games on TV or video.

- Once your teen gets an idea of how to play, take them to the tennis court; hand them a tennis racquet and a ball, and encourage them to play the game.

- At the outset, teach the teen simple and slow ways to play the sport and gradually raise the difficulty level once you notice they are getting a hang of it.

- Once they are able to play, you can enroll them in a tennis club; this will help them practice the game with other players.

Take note of the various responses of the teen at each stage and with each instruction.

Important notes:

_____
_____
_____
_____
_____
_____
_____
_____

Household chores

The idea	It is common for teens with autism to have trouble grasping theories such as responsibility and sharing. You can help your child appreciate the ideas practically. The best way is to get them to assist you with chores around the house.
How it helps	<ul><li>*Improve* home maintenance</li><li>*Help with practical knowledge about responsibility*</li><li>*Improve the teen's sense of empathy, care, and sharing*</li></ul>
You will need	None
Type	Indoor activity

What to do:

- Begin by allotting meager tasks to the teen, such as passing something from the fridge, placing things in order, cleaning with a cloth, and so on.

- As they get comfortable doing things around, you could teach them to make their beds, set the table, clean around the house, and even help cook a small meal.

Community gardening participation

The idea	Nature is predicated to have healing powers. Community gardening, such as music, can be relaxing and also allows your teen with autism to socialize. Becoming a part of gardening projects will assist in boosting your teen's social skills and help them come in contact with nature in a better way than usual.
How it helps	• Help to develop social skills • Enhance sensory abilities
You will need	A set of gardening tools containing the following: • grass shears, • trowel, shovel, • hand fork, and • other gardening equipment.
Type	Outdoor activity

What to do:

- Begin by spending some time with your kid in your home garden, that is if you have one. You could plant seeds, water plants, or rake the fallen leaves.

- Make available a gardening tool kit to your teen with autism; buoy them up to actively take part in several gardening projects.

Take note of the various responses of the teen at each stage and with each instruction.

Important notes:

Role-play

The idea	*Role-play is a tremendous tool that can help your teenager with autism practice social skills. It can aid with teaching the teen how to behave in different social situations with role-playing games and activities.*
How it helps	- *Helps develop social skills* - *Introduces the teen to social norms*
You will need	- *A list of situations* - *A script to teach them how to behave in that situation* - *Events that your teen is likely to encounter*
Type	*Indoor activity*

What to do:

- Begin by role-playing simple, basic scenes such as an interaction with an assistant at the supermarket.

- Once the teen gets a hang of the activity, you can move on to other social situations comprising more people. It is recommended that you pose as a different person each time; this will help the teen better understand that not everyone is the same.

- Role-plays can be an effective tool for teaching the teen how to interact with their classmates, friends, and teachers at school.

> **Take note of the various responses of the teen at each stage and with each instruction.**
>
> **Important notes:**
> _____
> _____
> _____
> _____
> _____
> _____
> _____
> _____
> _____

Chapter 4

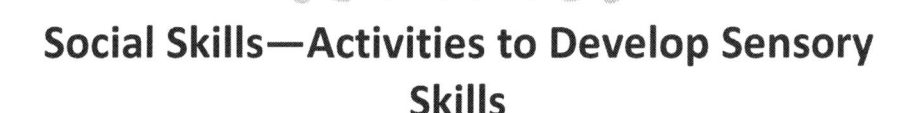

Social Skills—Activities to Develop Sensory Skills

Typically, the sensory skills of teenagers with autism are far less developed compared to that of their neurotypical contemporaries. This implies that teens with autism are unable to function at the same level as average teenagers. Getting them to participate in these activities and games can help improve their sensory abilities.

A. Staring Contest

The idea	*Healthy and efficient communication is predicated upon having eye contact. It depicts buoyancy and plays a key role in situations such as interviews and even dates. It is common for teens with autism to feel very uncomfortable with looking at other people in the eye. You can help them change that with this activity.*
How it helps	• *Helps them make healthy, appropriate eye contact* • *Increases self-confidence*

You will need	<ul><li>*A list of situations*</li><li>*A script to teach them how to behave in that situation*</li><li>*Events that your teen is likely to encounter*</li></ul>
Type	*Indoor activity*

What to do:

- Begin by sitting opposite your teenager with autism; ask them to look into your eyes.

- Request that they maintain contact as long as they possibly can. At first, the kid might be able to hold their gaze for a short period, maybe more than a few seconds, and that's OK.

- Continue playing the game as many times as you can. You can applaud them each time they succeed in holding their gaze for longer.

- As you make progress, it is important to also enlighten the teen about the difference between healthy eye contact and staring.

Take note of the various responses of the teen at each stage and with each instruction.

Important notes:

_____

_____

_____

_____

_____

_____

_____

_____

B. Spot the Difference

The idea	Even though kids with autism have strong visual skills, they typically lack the capacity to look for subtle variances. You can help them make the most of their visual skills and improve their attention to detail with this game.
How it helps	• Stimulates their visual sense • Encourages visual discrimination • Improves attention to details

You will need	<ul><li>*A set of spot the difference games*</li><li>*Sheets*</li><li>*Newspaper cuttings*</li></ul>
Type	Indoor activity

What to do:

- Begin with a simple *spot the difference* games you can find in the papers. Show the teen how it is played, and let them try the next one.

- Allow the teen to take as much time and as many attempts as they need while providing guidance at every step.

- Be careful not to reveal the answer to them; this will not only discourage them but defeat the aim of playing the game.

- Applaud the teen at each point when they spot a difference.

- You can add incentives to motivate them to play and think harder at solving each puzzle.

Take note of the various responses of the teen at each stage and with each instruction.

Important notes:

C. Emotion Simulations

The idea	In this game, Emotion Simulation, the teen with autism will have to express the emotion written on a piece of paper. Typically, teens with autism struggle to recognize emotions just by looking at other people. So to teach your kid to show any emotion, show them videos or photos of people with different expressions, and explain each of them.
How it helps	• Improves communication • Helps them in naming feelings

	• *Helps them in identifying and understanding expressions*
You will need	• *Pieces of paper* • *Timer*
Type	*Indoor activity*

What to do:

- You can play this game with family or your teen's buddies.

- Begin by playing the game yourself, showing how it is done. Encourage them to attempt identifying the emotion you are expressing.

- Ask your teen to pick a piece of paper as you did and try to express what is on the paper, without uttering a word.

> Take note of the various responses of the teen at each stage and with each instruction.

Important notes:

_____
_____
_____
_____
_____
_____
_____
_____
_____
_____
_____

D. Matching Game

The idea	*The matching game stimulates the brain, teaching your teen with autism to connect places, objects, events, and the like with their names, features, and more. You can try this game with emotions as well.*
How it helps	• *Improves connections to places, things, objects, and so on* • *Helps them with memory*

	• *Helps them with attention to detail*
You will need	• *Paper* • *Pictures of people displaying various emotions* • *Pictures of places, events, objects, etc.*
Type	*Indoor activity*

What to do:

- Begin by laying the photos on the table.

- Fold the pieces of paper into folded chits, and place them in a hamper.

- Ask your teen to pick up one piece of paper and try finding the matching photo.

- Applaud the teen every time they get one right.

- You can also play this as a group game; you can pair your teen having autism with a friend or family member.

Take note of the various responses of the teen at each stage and with each instruction.	

Important notes:

_____

_____

_____

_____

_____

_____

_____

_____

E. Watching TV Programs

The idea	*Empirical research has shown that kids with autism can benefit meaningfully from well-chosen TV programs. First of all, TV can open the world to your child; there, they can learn language skills which help them get familiar with topics that they can discourse with their peers. Additionally, TV programs can also aid them in learning how to behave in different social circumstances.*
How it helps	• *Stimulates visual and auditory senses*

	• *Develops language skills*
	• *Improves social skills*
You will need	• *TV*
	• *A few preselected TV programs*
Type	*Indoor activity*

What to do:

- Begin by allowing the teen to pick a video from your selection, and play that.

- Watch the program together.

- Ask questions in between to see if they are following; the questions should be about what is happening in the program. Make sure their questions are aired and answered as well.

- Even though the activity is about learning, make sure you do not become rigid about it. Make sure your kid is having fun too.

Take note of the various responses of the teen at each stage and with each instruction.

Important notes:

_____

_____

_____

_____

_____

_____

_____

_____

_____

_____

_____

Chapter 5

Social Skills Continued

A. Games That Involve Taking Turns

One of the disabilities that kids with autism face is their inability to appreciate order or organization. That is why they struggle to behave appropriately when they are told to wait for their turn. One of the most effective ways to teach them about order is through games and activities that involve turn-taking.

Board games

The idea	*Generally, children struggle to grasp the idea behind taking turns, as it is not an inherent skill that they possess. Learning about it is all the more problematic for kids with autism, who do not comprehend verbal explanations as much. Board games are the best examples of games to play with teenagers with autism.*
How it helps	• *Stimulates visual and auditory senses* • *Introduces them to concepts of rules and taking turns* • *Improves focus and attention to details*

You will need	• *Easy board games such as the following:* • *Snakes and Ladders* • *Ludo* • *Monopoly*
Type	Indoor activity

What to do:

- Begin by playing basic games that require nothing more than throwing the dice and moving the pawns.

- You should use words such as "your turn" and "my turn"; this will aid the teen in understanding the idea better.

- Be preemptive in giving the dice back to the other players after you have had a turn. This action would encourage your teen with autism to imitate you.

Take note of the various responses of the teen at each stage and with each instruction.

Important notes:

_____

_____

_____

_____

_____

_____

_____

_____

Playing with a car or playing catch

The idea	This activity is very simple, especially for teenagers with autism. If your teen has a hard time appreciating the idea of taking turns with board games, this game would be a good place to start.
How it helps	• Teaches about taking turns • Encourages patience
You will need	• Pull-back motor car toys
Type	Indoor activity

What to do:

- Begin by pairing up with your teen; sit opposite each other at either end of the room.

- Play with the car, taking turns to send it to each other.

- If your teen does not want to play with a car, you could try playing catch.

> Take note of the various responses of the teen at each stage and with each instruction.

Important notes:

_____
_____
_____
_____
_____
_____
_____
_____
_____
_____

B. Creative Activities for Teenagers with Autism

Parts of our daily lives are colors, shapes, and materials; creative activities give teenagers with autism the opportunity to discover these various elements, which inevitably prompt their sensory experience.

Paint with ice

The idea	*A combination of ice and color can be a very attractive piece of plaything that your teen with autism would not want to let go of. When your child paints with ice, he will see color and touch something "cold."*
How it helps	• *Engages the teenager physically and mentally* • *Encourages imagination*
You will need	• *Ice tray* • *Water* • *Watercolor or paints* • *Craft sticks* • *Paper*
Type	Indoor activity

What to do:

- Begin by helping your child combine water paints and water; pour the mixture into the ice tray.

- Place the craft sticks in the center, in a way that ensures they are standing; this would make it much easier to hold the frozen paint cubes.

- Once the paint cubes freeze over, take them out and let your teen pick a few preferred colors they intend on using.

- Hand them a paper and ask them to use the paint cubes to draw or paint something on the paper.

> Take note of the various responses of the teen at each stage and with each instruction.

Important notes:
_____
_____
_____
_____
_____
_____
_____
_____
_____

Storytelling invention

The idea	One challenge for children with autism is the ability to think along logical or rational lines. However, they possess an imagination that you can help improve. One way to do that is through unrehearsed storytelling activities.
How it helps	- Advances their imagination - Inspires them to be impulsive and ingenious - The right words of inspiration also lift their confidence
You will need	A list of ideas or plot that the children can build on such as - My day at school - A fun day at the mall - An adventure with my friend
Type	Indoor or outdoor activity

What to do:

- Gather your teen's friends in a circle. Storytelling invention is an activity that works great with groups.

- Ask one person to begin the story using a single sentence, such as, *"I went to the library today and..."*

- The next person should then complete that line and add it to the story.

- Encourage them all to say what readily comes to their minds.

- You can permit them to build the story as they desire; do not pose any form of evaluation. This will help in building their confidence.

> **Take note of the various responses of the teen at each stage and with each instruction.**
>
> **Important notes:**
> _____
> _____
> _____
> _____
> _____
> _____
> _____
> _____
> _____

iii. Crafts with clay

The idea	It can be disastrous to assume that all teens with autism like to get their hands dirty. However, if your kid is OK with it, creating crafts with clay is an activity they might enjoy. Right now, let's learn to make a simple snowflake sculpture with clay.
How it helps	• Helps develop creativity and the sense of touch • Enables them to use their hands to create something easily
You will need	• Air-dry clay, white • Clay modeling tools or snowflake molds
Type	Indoor activity

What to do:

- Typically, what is taught visually stays with teenagers with autism more than what is merely spoken. So explain that no two snowflakes are alike.

- Set a table with the clay, mold, and modeling tools.

- Begin by encouraging the teens to create a snowflake sculpture with the mold.

- Then encourage them to roll the clay into thin strands and make a snowflake using the tools.

- Remind them about what the snowflake looked like. They can make as many snowflakes as they possibly can, in various ways.

- Ensure that your teen isn't allergic or doesn't display acute irritation to clay before introducing them to this activity. Doing this would help avoid making their aversion stronger.

> Take note of the various responses of the teen at each stage and with each instruction.
>
> **Important notes:**
> _____
> _____
> _____
> _____
> _____
> _____
> _____
> _____
> _____

C. Picking the Right Activities

It is not enough to simply gather a list of activities and venture into trying them. This can be counterproductive in so many ways. It might be true that the above-listed activities are for teenagers with autism; however, this doesn't make every one of them suitable for your teen.

- It is important to ponder on the kind of skills your teen requires in order to develop: whether they are social skills, sensory skills, or motor skills. Again, ask yourself if the teen simply needs a dose of confidence.

- It is important to select games tailored to bring the anticipated result as regards behavioral changes, sensory stimulation, and so on.

- In the event that you select a group activity, ensure that you choose participants that your child is comfortable with. Likewise, include people who you reckon can aid your teen in developing their skills.

- It is important to reflect on any possible challenges you might encounter with your child during the activity. It is possible that your teen might not respond as anticipated, particularly if the activity prompts any noteworthy deviations in routine or breeds sensory overload.

- It is important to seek games and activities that match your teen's interests. Your child would be keen on being a part of an activity if they like it.

Irrespective of what activity you pick out, it is probable that you may end up encountering challenges with a teenager with autism, or you may be lucky enough not to have any issues at all. In any case, you would be better off not losing your patience. Go ahead and attempt these activities or others you know of as many times as you possibly can. As you put in the effort and allow time to take its course, you would be helping your teenager advance the skills they need for a smooth and comfortable life ahead.

Chapter 6

Friendship Skills

It is a fact that some of the most difficult skills to master are social skills; they are also particularly challenging to develop and deploy for use in the real world. These inevitably have clear repercussions, especially when it has to do with nurturing relationships with others.

Individuals with ASDs are prone to overly share information, experience a resilient sense of social nervousness, and, on occasion, have trouble appreciating body language and other elusive social cues. These are but a few of the impediments children and adults with autism can meet when nurturing friendships.

Teens with autism can probably feel sequestered at school on a daily basis; oftentimes than not, they need assistance in developing the social skills to make friends, which is a key part of the teen's unspoken curriculum, which denotes skills that kids need to develop separately from an academic environment. Statistics from the National Autistic Society indicate that at least 40 percent of children on the autism spectrum get bullied at school. Furthermore, 63 percent of the parents of children with autism are not convinced that their child's school offers adequate support for their wards.

Expectedly, by the teen or even pre-teen years, the concept of including everyone in family activities would no longer be the norm, parents can no longer arrange playdates as their kids begin to fragment themselves into diverse peer groups, often being a factor of common interests. With these, it becomes increasingly clear why teens with autism who had nurtured sturdy interests that may be out of the conventional for people their age may have difficulty finding someone who shares in their fascinations.

Furthermore, the trademarks of an ASD diagnosis are deficiencies in social skills and language abilities. However, these are the very tools so required to make teen friends. Teenage dialogues go further than what is spoken or can be heard. They count on more elusive forms of language, like body language, facial expressions, and speech nuances. They require having the ability to take the perspective of another, deduce, and ponder the thoughts and emotions of others. Trouble picking up on these social signals can lead to social slip-ups, misinterpretations, and possibly refutation, isolation, and bullying.

Friendships in teenagers can get further complicated due to co-occurring conditions common for people on the spectrum. In actuality, nervousness can make it challenging for your teen to try to make friends, mainly if they have had trouble in the past. Unanticipated behaviors such as throwing tantrums or unrestrained emotions may make peers cautious over getting to know your teen.

A. Why Friendships Are Important for Teenagers

Robust friendships assist teenagers in developing social and emotional fortitude. With each growth and maturity of such friendships, the teens get a healthy boost to their self-esteem and confidence. Having a shoulder to lean on can be as good as medicine in some cases. In addition, having friends also gives your kid experience in handling emotions, rejoining to the feelings and emotions of others, negotiating, cooperating, and problem-solving.

Teens with ASD are likely to have it tough when developing friendships. This is not unconnected to their having trouble with

- initiating and sustaining conversations.
- figuring out what other people are thinking and feeling.
- partaking in the activities of other teens.
- grasping facial expressions and body languages.
- acclimatizing to new social circumstances.
- coming up with quick solutions to social problems, such as how to sort out disagreements.

It is important for teenagers with ASD to be able to develop skills in these areas if their friendship skills are anything to go by.

B. Results of the Study on Autism and Friendship Skills

Recent studies on the relationship between activity participation, friendship, and internalizing problems in teenagers with autism pointed out the following:

- On the subject of activities, 62 percent of the kids partook in at least one supplementary sport or club.

- An estimated more than half of the children with ASD did not have a single close friend.

- Kids who partook in more sports, leisure pursuits, and clubs were more likely to have at least one friend. Furthermore, taking part in more activities was linked with more friends.

- Not a single direct relationship was found between friendships and internalizing problems.

- Not a single noteworthy relationship exists between activities and internalizing behaviors.

- IQ was strongly linked with friendship; average IQ was linked with having at least one friend and partaking in more sports and clubs.

- Better abilities to internalize problems were linked with higher IQ.

C. Helping Your Child with Autism Spectrum Disorder

There are a number of ways to assist your teen with ASD in learning positive social skills.

Be a role model.

Being a role model is taking the time out to always pave the way for your child as far as habits and actions are concerned by first displaying those habits and actions yourself. Your kid will learn a lot of key skills about friendship from watching you interrelate positively with others. Once you make it a habit of displaying to your teen the kind of social behaviors you desire to see, you inspire them to be like you. You can model skills such as listening, showing empathy, problem-solving abilities, and working through conflicts.

The key to being a role model is consistency. It isn't enough to be a role model every other day, when it is convenient, or when you are having a good day. As a parent, you have to make up your mind to be all your kid wants to be every day. Remember that your teen would need to see how you handle things like anger, disappointments, fear, excitement, and so on. Your words, actions, and inactions will mirror the kind of life that they might choose to emulate.

Answer the following questions as sincerely as you can.

a. *How often do you pose as a role model to your teen?*

*Always*_____   *When convenient*_____
*Never*_____

b. *How do you rate the value of role modeling in the mental development of your teen?*

*Highly*_____ *Not sure*_____ *Poorly*_____

c. *Can you mention areas where you have displayed role modeling to your teen for their emulation?*

_____

_____

_____

d. *How can you describe your teen's reaction when they noticed your role modeling and emulated?*

_____

_____

_____

In addition, it will help a lot if you explain to your child the skills you're modeling. For instance, to encourage sharing and turn-taking, you might say, "I'm going to be friendly and share my toy car with you," or "I'm going to have a turn on the swing. Your turn next."

Help your child develop basic social skills

The fact remains that for a teen with ASD, a lot of essential social skills for making friends need to be taught, including the ability to say hello, take turns, share, and make compromises. One of the best ways to help your teen learn these skills is by practicing social skills at home with them.

You can also adopt the use of social stories in teaching social skill development. This method is known to be very effective in teaching your teen skills like communication and joining in with others. Every turn should be explored by you to further groom the social skills of your teen. With every move, their capacity would be enlarged in no time.

Answer the following questions as sincerely as you can.

a. *How often do you deliberately develop the social skills of your teen?*

Always_____ When convenient_____Never_____

b. *Can you mention a few basic social skills that you would want to see developed in your teen in the nearest future?*

_____

_____

_____

c. *What modalities have you put in place to help your teen grow the skills listed above?*

_____

_____

_____

Recognize and praise your child's success.

Due to the nature of teens with ASD being emotionally fragile, they require a lot of commendation and encouragement whenever they do something right. Negative reactions have a way of turning them off any topic or project. So, when you see them interacting positively with others, waiting patiently in line, or not interrupting others, commend them. A few words of assurance would go a long way in boosting their confidence and helping them continue along the path they are on.

In addition, you can take it a step further by rewarding their good behavior. Such rewards are incentives for good behavior and would help them keep the good work going. Rewards can vary from snacks to added TV time to reductions in chores.

Answer the following questions as sincerely as you can.

a. How often do you deliberately praise and encourage your teen?

Always_____ When convenient_____ Never_____

b. Can you mention areas where you have openly praised or commended your teen?

_____

_____

_____

c. What modalities have you put in place to help you continually praise, commend, and encourage your teen?

_____

_____

_____

Chapter 7

Friendship Skills—Developing Friendships

Your child may benefit from counseling to learn social skills, overcome anxiety, and learn to regulate their behaviors. But aside from having a really good behavior plan and Individualized Education Program (IEP) and filling the week with social skills groups, what can your teen do to develop friendships?

A. Initiate and Reciprocate

It is important to state that it takes a friend to be a friend. In most cases, your teen may need to be the one to make the first move, as far as forming a friendship is concerned. You can encourage the kid to initiate social interaction, even though it may be uncomfortable for them.

This may begin by simply saying, "Hi" to people in the hallway at school and inquiring about their weekend, talking about the forthcoming Algebra test, or remarking on the school lunch offerings. Furthermore, your teen must be ready for other people's responses and rejoinders; when someone talks to them, they need to know how to respond appropriately.

As a parent, you can create scenarios for practice at home for your child. This will help them get used to initiating conversations with and around people they know before they step out into the real world.

EXERCISE

- *Have a conversation with your teen about friendships and the importance of sometimes taking the first steps by initiating conversation.*

- *Ask about, and allow the teen to express their fears and challenges when it comes to initiating conversations with others. Some hindrances might be*

    - *fear of the unknown;*

    - *anxiety;*

    - *not knowing what to say; and*

    - *not wanting to make a mistake and be laughed at.*

- *Assure them that even though their fears might be possible, gaining a new friend is also possible and should be explored.*

- *Create various scenes at different times in the day in which your teen is placed in the position to initiate conversation.*

- *Encourage your teen to employ various etiquettes while holding a conversation. For instance, let them smile; let them say "please"; let them pay compliments where required; and so on.*

- *Once your teen gets back home from school, you should find time to have a discussion on how their day went and whether or not they initiated any conversation or made any new friends that day. Encourage them to do more as the need arises.*

> **Take note of the various responses of the teen at each stage and with each instruction.**

Important notes:

_____
_____
_____
_____
_____
_____
_____
_____
_____

B. Get Involved

Being a part of a group of a school-based organization can greatly help your teen improve their friendship skills. Therefore, embolden them to join clubs or organizations at school and in your community. You might even want to consider having your teen find a few after-school activities to be part of. Besides, if your teen comes home and drops in front of the TV or computer every day, the chances of developing friendship would be exceedingly limited. You can assist your kid in looking for something that they are genuinely interested in.

If your teenager likes sports, have them join a team, even if it is them being part of the managerial arm or working the numbers (statistician). It is a fact that team sports can occasionally be challenging to learn in the teenage years, but sports such as tennis and squash have developmental leagues for people of all ages, which may assist your teen in meeting new people and even developing a healthy new passion.

If sports aren't your teen's passion, perhaps it might be dancing, robotics, or computers. Your local YMCA and/or community college would probably have an array of classes to choose from if there isn't something available at your teen's school. In addition, your local church or synagogue would likely have a youth group with a plan and supervised activities too.

EXERCISE

- *Have a conversation with your teen about friendships and the importance of being a part of a group or an organization.*

- *Ask about, and allow the teen to express their fears and challenges when it comes to joining groups in school or the community. Some hindrances might be*
    - *fear of the unknown;*
    - *anxiety;*
    - *not knowing how to go about it; and*

- *○ not finding the right group that meets their interests.*

- *Assure them that even though their fears might be real, joining a group has much more benefits than they could enjoy.*

- *Take time to visit your teen's school and inquire about available groups.*

- *Collaborate with your teen, their teachers, and school authority to select a group that best meets the interests of the kid.*

Take note of the various responses of the teen at each stage and with each instruction.

Important notes:

_____

_____

_____

_____

_____

_____

_____

_____

_____

C. Encourage Age-Appropriate Activities When Possible

It is possible to have your teen sustain a keen but unhealthy interest in activities that other kids their age have long outgrown. This can be saddening for any parent and can indicate a slowed pace of development in the teen. You can handle this challenge by making a deal with your teen. Your kid can go to their preferred group if they try something new (cooking, for instance). In the event where your teen is not developmentally prepared for a group of the same age and typical peers, you can look for a special needs group that your kid can join.

Inasmuch as you would want to enlarge your child's perspectives, you must be careful not to put your child in a situation that is too much for them to handle. You can begin with what is comfortable and branch out from there where necessary. The idea is for your child to have the occasion to practice social skills and develop friendships. What is central is that your teen experiences success, irrespective of the setting.

EXERCISE

- *Have a conversation with your teen about friendships and the importance of being a part of age-appropriate groups and activities.*
- *Ask about, and allow the teen to express their fears and challenges when it comes to joining groups in school or the community. Some hindrances might be*
  o *fear of the unknown;*

- *anxiety;*
- *feeling unskilled enough to join age-appropriate groups; and*
- *not finding the right group that meets their interests.*

- *Assure them that even though their fears might be real, joining age-appropriate groups has much more benefits than they could enjoy.*
- *Make a deal with them to allow them to do activities they enjoy (even though not age-appropriate) if they agree to try doing other age-appropriate activities.*
  - *Make a schedule, and have it implemented.*

> **Take note of the various responses of the teen at each stage and with each instruction.**

Important notes:

_____
_____
_____
_____
_____
_____
_____
_____
_____

D. Blend In

Every kid has an individuality that must be nurtured and respected. Exhibiting such uniqueness in how they speak, dress, or see life is key for their mental and physical growth. However, it is important to act and look like everybody else, blending in seamlessly. This keeps the teen away from unnecessary attention that might lead to teasing and bullying.

Your teen might have no issue with whatever they choose to wear out, but their peers at school will notice and judge in view of that. It is therefore important to pay close attention to the fashion trends at the moment and how they are being worn.

For instance, take note of how low kids wear their pants on their waists, how long they keep their hair, what type of shoes they prefer even on formal occasions, if they prefer to wear graphic t-shirts of popular bands or collared shirts, jeans or khakis, carry a backpack or use a rolling cart.

Remember that the motive behind blending in isn't to obstruct your teen's individuality but to protect it from hostilities that exist out there. You can make a deal with your kid to at least try out a few outfits or fashion styles every other day.

EXERCISE

- *Have a conversation with your teen about friendships and the importance of blending in.*

- *Ask about, and allow the teen to express their fears and challenges when it comes to blending in. Some hindrances might be*
- *fear of the unknown;*
- *anxiety;*
- *the feeling of being caged in; and*
- *allergic reactions to some clothing materials or serious aversions to the scent of particular colognes.*
- *Assure them that even though their fears might be real, blending in has much more benefits than they could enjoy.*
  - *Make a deal with them to allow them to wear whatever they prefer if they agree to try out other popular fashion trends every other day.*

> **Take note of the various responses of the teen at each stage and with each instruction.**
>
> **Important notes:**
>
> _____
>
> _____
>
> _____
>
> _____
>
> _____
>
> _____
>
> _____
>
> _____

E. Practice Good Hygiene

It is important to teach your child the association between cleanliness and establishing a friendship. They need to know that being ignored, shunned, or worse is what they would probably get if they have terrible hygiene, such as body odor or bad breath. You can help out by ensuring that healthy hygiene habits are regularized in the kid's life. You can set up various ways to remind them. Make sure your teen takes regular showers, brushes their hair, wears deodorant, doesn't wear too much cologne or perfume, and practices good grooming skills daily.

EXERCISE

- *Have a conversation with your teen about friendships and the importance of good hygiene.*

- *Ask about and allow the teen to express their fears and challenges when it comes to hygiene. Some hindrances might be*

    - *dislike for certain elements, such as water;*

    - *anxiety;*

    - *worn out tools, such as a bad toothbrush; and*

    - *allergic reactions to some clothing materials or serious aversions to the scent of particular colognes.*

- *Assure them that you will make arrangements to help them maintain good hygiene as far as it depends on you.*

- *Craft out a reminder to help them remember to do certain things at certain times, such as washing their hands immediately after they come home or brushing their teeth before leaving the house.*

> **Take note of the various responses of the teen at each stage and with each instruction.**
>
> **Important notes:**
>
> _____
>
> _____
>
> _____
>
> _____
>
> _____
>
> _____
>
> _____
>
> _____

F. Know What's Trending

It is important for you as a parent to always be on the lookout for what is currently trending and popular so that you can expose your child to it. This will give your teen something to talk about or support when they join in a conversation with peers. You can begin by watching popular movies and TV shows with your kid; while at it, make sure you explain any uncharted content. It is possible to be a bit concerned that a popular show is too unconventional for your ward, but you have to know that if it is popular with their age group, your kid will become exposed to it sooner rather than later.

EXERCISE

- *Have a conversation with your teen about friendships and the importance of what is trending and popular.*

- *Ask about and allow the teen to express their fears and challenges exploring what is popular. Some hindrances might be*

    - *fear of the unknown;*
    - *anxiety; and*
    - *not being skilled enough to follow or discuss the trend.*

- *Assure them that their fears are noted, but they should not stop them from exploring.*

- *Come up with a list of trending or popular things together, and discuss how you all can explore them together.*

> Take note of the various responses of the teen at each stage and with each instruction.
>
> **Important notes:**
>
> _____
>
> _____
>
> _____
>
> _____
>
> _____
>
> _____
>
> _____
>
> _____
>
> _____

The most significant variable that determines whether or not your teen cultivates friendships is their aspiration to do so. Some teens with autism don't care much if they have a friend until they see a reason for having one, perhaps to have a girlfriend or a date to a school dance. Until that impetus, they are comfortable being alone. Besides, friendship is hard work: it involves sharing, compromising, showing interest in someone else's passions, and being thoughtful of someone else's feelings. Being able to be a friend as well as having one doesn't happen overnight. Remind yourself and your child that friendship is a process, not an end in itself.

Chapter 8

Friendship Skills

A. Autism Spectrum Disorder and Bullying

Bullying is when young kids tease other kids over and over again. It can also be when they tease with the intention of hurting the feelings of another person. Bullying can stretch to kids not wanting another kid to have fun or participate in games or activities with others. Bullying can range from saying mean things and calling people unpleasant names to spreading nasty stories about them, leaving people out of activities, hitting and pushing them, or forcefully taking their things.

Research indicates that children and teens with ASD stand a higher risk of bullying, particularly in conventional schools. They are more likely to be the target of this gruesome act compared to their peers. Bullying does a lot of damage to the self-esteem, mental health, social skills, and overall academic progress of its victim. The reason why this category of kids gets bullied the most is that children who bully others are likely to pick on children who are quiet, shy, and who lack friendship skills. Bullies also have a habit of picking on children who conduct themselves differently or who have unique interests, trends, and styles different from themselves and other children the same age.

Children with ASD typically do not know how to go about joining in a group and therefore act in inappropriate ways, such as struggling, aggressively seeking attention, or dominating. Such actions are bound to trigger annoyance from other children, which could deteriorate into physical or verbal clashes with peers. Also, it mostly is challenging for children with ASD to figure out who are the good guys and who are the bad guys. This implies that before they make out who the bullies are, they might already have been hurt over and over by them in the playground. They might also tend to believe what they're told, such as, "If you do this, I'll be your friend."

EXERCISE

Have a chat with your teen about the subject of bullying.

- *Ask if they have ever been bullied in school or the community.*

- *Ask how they felt and how they reacted.*

- *Ask how they were able to wrinkle themselves out of the situation.*

- *Ask what led to the bullying; did they say something to attract the bully?*

- *Ask if it has affected how they make friends in school.*

- *Ask what they wish could be done to help them overcome bullying*

> **Take note of the various responses of the teen at each stage and with each instruction.**

Important notes:

_____

_____

_____

_____

_____

_____

_____

_____

_____

B. Signs That a Teenager with Autism Is Being Bullied

It is often a challenge to spot bullying, particularly for a teen with autism. There are a number of reasons for this occurrence. First, the teen might have limited speech or not know how to communicate their experiences. Second, the teen might not always recognize when they're being bullied, mostly when the bullying is more indirect. And sometimes, the teen with autism might think a child is bullying them when the child is only just trying to chat or play with them. Trying to ascertain whether a teen with autism is being bullied can indeed be tough. The way kids respond to such occurrences is subject to the nature and severity of the bullying, as well as to their dispositions. However, there are some signs you can keep an eye out for in your child with autism.

Signs	Observations
Physical signs	*Your teen might* • *have inexplicable bruises, wounds, and scratches.* • *come home with missing or damaged possessions or outfits.* • *come home hungry.*
Behavioral signs	*Your teen might* • *be increasingly hesitant about going to school.* • *be scared of walking or catching the bus to school.* • *begin to perform poorly at school.*
Emotional signs	*Your teen might* • *have increased nightmares.* • *cry a lot.* • *get overly aggressive.* • *have mood swings.* • *not want to talk about what's on their mind.* • *feel apprehensive.*

	• *seem withdrawn.* • *begin to stammer.*
Other signs	*Your teen might* • *say they feel sick or have a stomachache.* • *have fluctuations in their eating or sleeping patterns.* • *begin to bully others.*

C. Speaking to Teenagers with Autism about Bullying

Suspecting that your teen is being bullied is one thing; however, the best way to know for sure is to have a conversation with your teen about bullying. Once you know more, thereby establishing whether or not they are being bullied, you can take action with the school and help your child to handle bullying. Moreover, having calm and caring conversations with you will also help your teen feel love and support.

You could begin by asking your kid whether something or someone has made them unhappy. If your teen has limited speech, drawing pictures, or pointing to pictures or drawings to show you what's bothering them can be a good way to have them express themselves. One innovative and helpful thing you can do is to develop an emotional timeline. This chart can help you determine how your child was feeling during different activities in the day. An emotion timeline can be a listing of the day's events in sequential order. Give your kid pictures of printed emoji faces of various emotions, such as happy, sad, angry, and so on. Beginning at the start of the day, say the name of the activity, and get your child to pick the face that expresses how they were feeling at that time.

D. Collaborating with Schools on Bullying

It is important to solicit the assistance of your teen's school as quickly as you can if you establish that your teen is being bullied. These days, schools take bullying very seriously; and expectedly, your teen's teachers will be trained in spotting and handling the unpleasant act. They'll work with you to try to stop further bullying.

You can begin by setting up a meeting with your teen's teacher, the school administration, the school welfare coordinator, or specialist support staff. Since the focus is getting results, it is expected that you, the parent, would choose to express your concerns calmly enough so that the meeting can go well. This means you have to preplan your every word before going into the meeting.

At the meeting, you can explicate how the concerns are upsetting your child, and get the school's standpoint on the matter. By collaborating with school staff, you can easily ascertain the times, places, students, and activities that are more in the cards to put your child at risk of bullying. Furthermore, you can inquire about the school's approaches for handling and averting bullying. For instance, it might have

- safe lunchtime choices for children, such as the library, chess, or gardening clubs.

- overseen safe places for children to go to if they need to.

- a member of staff that teens know they can report bullying too, and a bully box to use if they don't want to speak to someone.

- a program to encourage awareness of autism.

- programs to assist children with autism to advance play and social skills.

- cooperative group activities that include children with autism socially.

- a buddy system.

Before the meeting comes to an end, ensure you have a plan on how you and the school are going to manage the situation.

E. Supporting Teenagers with Autism at Home

The fact is that teens with autism require support and love at home if they are experiencing bullying at school. Your kid also needs to recognize that the state of affairs at the moment is not their fault at all and that they have your assurance of sorting it out. Furthermore, it is central to help your teen appreciate what bullying is; you could use social stories, role-play, or cartoon strips to illustrate to them the difference between bullying and accidents or misapprehensions.

It's also imperative for your teen to be able to get away from bullying. You could begin by giving them a list of rules to follow.

For instance, "Smile, talk, walk, and tell an adult."

Furthermore, you can craft out a prompt card to help remind your kid of what to do and whom to talk to if they ever are being bullied. Also, you could write down words for telling the teacher or a note to give to the teacher or put in the bully box. Ensure that your kid knows where the school's safe places are located. You could request or craft out a school map showing the safe places; this will help the teen visualize where to go.

In addition, working on your teen's social skills can assist them in knowing what to do in different scenarios, giving them ways to cope. For instance, you could make sure your teen knows to say "Stop! I don't like that" and to find a teacher if they're being bullied. Another way of raking in protection for your kid from bullying is through supportive friends. By organizing playdates or other social activities, you can help your child develop friendships with children at and outside school.

F. When Teenagers with Autism Are Bullying Others

It is possible for the social and emotional troubles teens with autism experience to lead them toward behaving like bullies. A few things can be done if you suspect your child is bullying others:

- Ensure your kid realizes what bullying is. You can help them see that calling people names or discriminating against them could be bullying.

- Ascertain what is causing the problem and why your teen is behaving this way. You might need to help your child find other ways to behave. For instance, you can request that an adult should help the teen join in activities. Your kid's class teacher, a specialist support teacher, or a psychologist could assist you with this.

- Talk to the school about its methods of antibullying. Ask what you can do from home to back this method. Call the school often to check how your teen is acting and to see what else you can do to help.

- Assist your teen in developing social skills. This will help your child comprehend social rules and how their behavior upsets others. Speak to the professionals who work with your teen about rehabilitations or supports that could help your teen.

- Reward your kid for positive social behavior like taking turns. And give clear penalties for bullying. For instance, if your teen isn't allowing someone else to join in, they might have to miss out on the activity.

G. Strategies for Handling Bullying

It is true that a lot is being done by individuals, groups, and local authorities to craft bully-free zones in schools. However, it is just as essential to equip our teens with handy approaches aimed at helping them in handling bullying. Here is an overview of some antibullying strategies.

1. Approaches for Handling Verbal Teasing

Inquiry:	*Response:*
What do most adults tell teens to do in response to teasing?	*Walk away, ignore them, tell an adult*

Problem:

If you inquire of a teen if these approaches work, the response would likely be in the negative.

Typically, the bully often keeps teasing, even when ignored by the teen or when they walk away. Reporting to an adult may earn the teen a label called "snitch"; this may inspire the bully to think and plan out some form of retaliation, and the cycle would continue.

<u>*Solution*</u>*:*

Use an organically effective social skill in its place. The teen should simply act like what the person said didn't trouble them and give a brief rejoinder that establishes their indifference, such as,

- *Whatever...*
- *So what?*
- *Who cares?*
- *Yeah, and?*
- *And your point is?*
- *Am I supposed to care?*
- *Is that supposed to be funny?*
- *Anyway...*

It is best to accompany these comebacks with a little eye-rolling or some shoulder shrugging, trailed by the teen hiking away or removing themselves from the situation when unimaginable. This approach guarantees that the teasing was not fun for the bully and makes it less probable that the teen will be teased yet again.

Even though this approach might do the job as far as handling verbal teasing from peers is concerned, this approach isn't recommended to be deployed with adults or teens who have a tendency to get violent.

2. Approaches for Handling Physical Teasing

Inquiry:	*Response:*
What do most adults tell teens to do in response to physical bullying?	*Report to an adult; fight back.*

Problem:

Reporting the incident to an adult can trigger the bully, as they might get in trouble over their actions; this would make them want to hit back.

Fighting back may end up getting one or all parties injured or get the teen in trouble.

<u>*Solution:*</u>

- *It is best to shun the bully while staying out of reach. Ensure not to draw attention to self when the bully is nearby.*
- *Do nothing to incite the bully. Do not stalk the bully, or tell on them for minor offenses.*
- *Don't tease or make fun of the bully.*
- *Don't deploy the approaches meant for handling verbal teasing as listed above; this might humiliate the bully and may result in violence.*
- *Do not attempt to make friends with the bully. This hardly is effective and may often end up in further harassment.*
- *Hang around other teens. Bullies prefer to pick on teens that are by themselves, as this makes them easy targets.*
- *Stay close to adults when the bully is around.*
- *If you're in jeopardy, seek help from an adult.*

Approaches for Handling Gossips and Rumors	
Inquiry: *What do most adults tell teens to do when they are the target of rumors or gossip?*	*Response:* *Confront the person and tell them how you feel, let everyone know that the rumor is untrue.*

Problem:

Confrontation isn't the best strategy, as confronting the person who is spreading the rumor and telling them how you feel will only generate more gossip.

You can also certainly not refute a rumor or gossip. Telling others the rumor is untrue will simply make you look defensive and will typically result in more gossip.

<u>*Solution*</u>*:*

- *Don't confront the person(s) spreading the gossip. This will generate more gossip, increase the intensity of the rumor mill, and may result in the bully wanting to hit back further.*

- *Shun the person(s) spreading the gossip when possible, as the bully and others are likely looking forward to a confrontation. Don't generate more attention and gossip by going close to them.*

- *Act startled that anyone would accept as true or care about the rumor. When the topic comes up in a conversation, make statements like, "Can you believe anyone cares about that?" "I can't believe anyone would believe that" or "People need to find something better to talk about."*

- *Admit the rumor to those you trust in front of those who might overhear; then emasculate its significance and/or validity. Do not try to invalidate the rumor, as this hardly ever works and may make you look self-justifying. In its place, do the following:*

- *First admit the rumor by saying something like, "Did you hear this rumor about me?" Do this with someone you trust that will support you, while in front of others who will overhear what you're saying.*

- *Then discredit the significance or validity of the rumor by saying something like, "Can you believe anyone would believe that or even care? People need to get a life and find something better to talk about. That's so lame." This will take the power out of the rumor and make others who spread it feel less important.*

- *If done correctly, the new rumor will be how little you care about the old rumor and how lame it was in the first place.*

Chapter 9

Friendship Skills—Peer Pressure and Peer Influence on Teenagers with Autism

Peer pressure is the uninterrupted influence on people by peers; it is the influence on an individual who is invigorated and desires to follow their peers by changing their attitudes, values, or behaviors to fit into those of the influencing group or individual. Peer influence is when an individual chooses to do something that they otherwise would not do, simply because they want to feel accepted and esteemed by their friends. Most times, the definition of peer pressure or influence isn't always bordered around doing something against the person's will.

Peer influence is known to be one of the foremost ways to describe how teenagers' behavior is fashioned by desiring to feel they belong to a group of friends or peers. However, peer pressure and influence when properly channeled can yield some measure of positivity. For instance, your teen might be influenced to become more assertive, try new activities, or get more involved with the school. In the same vein, it can be negative too. Teenagers might decide on trying things they typically wouldn't be interested in, like smoking or behaving in rebellious ways.

Peer pressure and influence might result in children

- deciding to wear clothing, hairstyle, or pieces of jewelry that is similar to that of their friends.

- deciding to listen to a music genre or watch TV shows that are similar to what their friends are listening or watching, respectively.

- deciding to alter the way they talk or their choice of words.

- deciding to embark on hazardous adventures or break rules.

- deciding to work harder at school or not work as hard.

- deciding to date or take part in sexual activities.

- deciding to smoke or use alcohol or other drugs.

A. Finding a Balance for Peer Pressure and Peer Influence

The concern for parents usually is that their teen is being excessively influenced by their peers or that the teen is throwing out their values, which their parents painstakingly built into them to fit in with their friends. Another concern for parents is that the teen might not be able to say no if they get pressured to try hazardous things, like shunning school or smoking.

The fact is that teens listening to a similar genre of music and sharing the same fashion sense as their friends do isn't tantamount to them doing antisocial or risky things. Furthermore, if the teen is content with who they are, their newfound choices, and values, they are less likely to be influenced by other people. The teen might decide to do some things that their friends do, but not others. The influence of the parent, however, is important as well; it is probably the biggest factor shaping the values and long-term choices of their kid.

With parental influence and a strong personality, it is more likely that the teen will know where to draw the line when it comes to peer pressure and influence.

Exercise

Answer the following questions:

1. *Have you had any discussion with your teen about the concepts and realities of peer pressure and influence?*
   Yes _____   *No*

   _____

2. *What have been your greatest concerns for your teen with autism when it comes to being pressured or influenced?*

_____
_____
_____
_____
_____

3. *What are some of the modalities you have put in place to help your teen stay in line and keep their values no matter what?*

_____
_____
_____
_____
_____

B. Helping Your Child Manage Peer Pressure and Peer Influence

Muddling through peer influence is about attaining the sense of balance right between being oneself and fitting in within their group. Here are some concepts to assist your teen with this.

Shape up your teen's self-esteem and confidence.

Studies indicate that teens who possess strong self-esteem are better at repelling negative peer pressure and influence. Self-esteem and confidence can be nurtured by inspiring your teen to try new things that give them an opportunity to succeed and to keep trying even when things are hard.

In addition, you can be a role model for confidence too, showing your kid how to act confident as the first step toward feeling confident. Also, take the time to shower praises on your teen for trying hard in building self-esteem and confidence.

Exercise

Answer the following questions:

1. *How do you rate the confidence level of your teen?*

    Low _____Average _____   Optimum

    _____

2. *How often do you set an example for them to follow in order to help their self-esteem and confidence?*

    *Rarely _____   When   convenient   _____
    Always _____*

3. *List a few activities that you can engage them in to help them improve their confidence.*

    _____
    _____
    _____
    _____
    _____

Always keep communication open.

Nurture a very lucid path of communication with your teen. Ensure that they are totally at home with telling you anything and everything going on with them. This will help you stay on top of the thing going on with them, and it will help you quickly notice changes that are unacceptable. If your kid feels more comfortable talking to you, they will not drift too far before you get them back on track.

Exercise

Answer the following questions:

1. *How do you rate the depth of communication that exists between you and your teen?*

    Shallow _____ Average _____

    Exceptional _____

2. *How often does your teen open up to you about what is happening around them?*

    Rarely _____ On occasion _____

    Often _____

3. *List down activities that you feel might help deepen your mutual communication with your teen.*

    _____
    _____
    _____
    _____
    _____

Propose ways to say no.

It is important for your kid to have some face-saving ways to say no if they are feeling influenced to do something they do not want to do. For instance, friends might be encouraging them to try smoking. Instead of them simply saying, "No, thanks," they could say, "No, it makes my asthma worse," or "No, I don't like the way it makes me smell."

The idea isn't to spoon-feed your teen with a bunch of lies to tell whenever they are under any kind of pressure. The goal is to teach them a quick way to decline going down the wrong path without necessarily lying or appearing weak to their peers. Standing their ground, however, is dependent on how grounded their self-esteem and confidence are in the first instance.

Exercise

1. *How often does your teen say no to what they do not want to do around the house?*

    Rarely _____ *Sometimes* _____

    Always _____

2. *How easily do they succumb to pressure to say yes?*

    Rarely _____ *Sometimes* _____

    Always _____

3. List ways for them to say no without sounding weak or afraid to their peers.

_____
_____
_____
_____
_____

Give teenagers a way out.

There is always a likelihood of your teen being in grave danger or a risky situation. You can advise them to text or call you for backup. You and your teen can come up with a coded message for those times when they don't want to feel embarrassed in front of friends. For instance, the kid could say that they are checking on a sick relative, whereas you would know that it indicates that they need a hand.

In the event where your teen does call you, ensure that you keep focusing on your kid's positive choice to ask you for help, rather than on the precarious situation your kid is in. Your teen is probably going to ask for help if they know they won't get into trouble for doing so.

Exercise

Answer the following questions:

1. How do you rate the depth of communication that exists between you and your teen?

Shallow _____ *Average* _____

Exceptional _____

2. *How often does your teen share code messages with you for help?*

    Rarely _____ *On occasion* _____

    Often _____

3. *List down activities that you feel might help deepen your mutual communication and coded ways for your child to ask for help without feeling embarrassed.*

    _____
    _____
    _____
    _____
    _____

C. Encourage a Wide Social Network

If your child has the opportunity to nurture friendships from many sources, comprising sport, family activities, or clubs, it will show that they have got lots of other options and sources of support if a friendship goes wrong.

D. When You're Concerned about Peer Pressure and Peer Influence

Inspiring your child to have friends over and giving them space in your home can aid you in getting to know your teen's friends. This also gives you the opportunity to assess whether or not negative peer pressure and influence are a concern for your kid. Good communication and a positive relationship with your teen might also inspire your kid to talk to you if they feel the negative influence from peers.

If you begin to nurse concerns that your teen's friends are a negative influence, criticizing them would only lead to your teen going to see them behind your back. If the kid figures that you do not accept their friends, they might even want to see more of them. So it's imperative to have a chat with them and listen without judging, gently helping your kid to see the influence their peers are having.

This might imply chatting with your teen about any behavior you might not fancy rather than the people you don't like. For instance, you might say, "When you're with your friends, you frequently get into fights." This can be better than saying, "You need to find new friends."

It can help to compromise with your child. For instance, letting them wear certain clothes or letting them have their hair cut in a precise fashion can help them feel attached to their peers, even if you are not keen on it. Letting your teen have some freedom can decrease the risk of more risky choices. Having friends and feeling attached to a group gives teenagers a sense of being accepted and being valued, which assists in developing self-esteem and confidence. Friendships also aid teenagers in absorbing important social and emotional skills, such as being sensitive to other people's thoughts, feelings, and well-being.

E. When to Be Concerned about Peer Influence and Peer Pressure

If you notice variations in the general mood of your teen, their behavior, eating, or sleeping patterns, which you suspect are due to their friends, it might be time to have a talk with them.

Some mood and behavioral alterations are normal in teenagers. But if your kid appears to be in a low mood for more than two weeks, or it gets in the way of things they usually relish, you might have to start worrying about your child's mental health.

Some warning signs include the following:

- low dispositions, tearfulness, or outlooks of desperateness
- hostility or antisocial behavior that's not typical for your child
- abrupt changes in behavior, often for no understandable reason
- trouble falling asleep, staying asleep, or waking early
- loss of appetite or overeating

- unwillingness to go to school

- withdrawal from activities your child used to like

- statements about wanting to give up or life not being worth living.

F. Children at Risk of Negative Peer Pressure and Influence

Some children are more in the offing to be negatively influenced by peers. These include children who

- have poor self-esteem.

- feel they have few friends.

- have special needs.

These children might feel that the only way they'll be included and accepted in social groups is by taking on the behavior, attitudes, and look of a group. Also, peer pressure or influence is strongest in early to middle adolescence. Boys are more likely to give in to peer pressure than girls.

Chapter 10

Life Skills

The growth and eventual independence of teens are inevitable, and at some point, we all have to make peace with such a reality. For parents with kids on the spectrum, this landmark can appear even more frightening. Some parents face an uphill task when simply dressing their wards up for the winter, and so teaching other life skills can appear overpowering. Moreover, the word "succeed" can be grossly disingenuous. This is because each kid with autism develops differently, making their measure of success unique. For some, wearing clothing, remembering to eat, or just being able to sail across daily tasks will be the goal. For others, it will be remembering to get to class or carrying out tasks at their jobs. Once these kids with autism hit adolescence and eventually adulthood, you would then begin to see some of the early work on life skills paying off in certain areas. In some areas, however, they might always need care.

Functional life skills are the everyday responsibilities we all need to lead self-governing lives. Mastering these skills forms self-esteem and confidence while achieving independence. Many people learn life skills via reflexive watching, imitation, or practicing a few times. But individuals with autism regularly need unambiguous instruction with many more reiterations to obtain the same skills. It is the duty of the parents to teach life skills so that their wards can make the most of their potential for full participation in everyday life.

For teens with autism, learning life skills is important to upsurge their independence at home, at school, and in the community. By familiarizing themselves with these skills early and building block by block, teens with autism acquire the tools that will allow them to boost their self-esteem and lead to more happiness in all areas of their lives.

A. What Are Life Skills?

Life skills, which are occasionally referred to as independent living skills or daily living skills, are a skill that we acquire to help us live life to the fullest without having to be dependent on anybody. Basic life skills comprise self-care activities, cooking, money management, shopping, room organization, and transportation. These skills are learned over time, starting at home at a very young age and developing further throughout adolescence and adulthood.

It is critical to learn a wide range of life skills that apply to many areas of life. It is also imperative to take in executive function skills or thinking skills such as organizing, planning, prioritizing, and decision-making related to each life skill being taught. Classifications of life skills include the following:

- Safety awareness

- Self-determination/advocacy

- Peer relationships, socialization, and social communication

- Community participation and personal finance

- Career path and employment

- Transportation

- Leisure/recreation

- Home living skills

B. Determining Which Life Skills to Teach

Teachers and psychoanalysts use formal valuations to determine which skills a child needs to learn. However, parents can carry out their informal assessments to successfully determine those needs.

Format	Methods
Formal assessments by professionals	a. Assessment of Functional Living Skills (AFLS) b. Assessment of Basic Language and Learning Skills (ABLLS)
Informal assessments made by parents	a. Ask your child which skills they would like to learn. b. Come up with a list of tasks where your child still needs support. c. Come up with a list of activities that would grow your child's individuality. d. Search for online checklists or chore charts grouped by age.* *Remember when looking at lists arranged by age range, your child may do better with teaching tailored to their developmental age.

C. Strategies for Teaching Life Skills

Knowing what needs to be imbibed into your kid is important, but it is one thing to know what is needed, while it is another thing to figure out how to go about imbibing what is required. There are a number of different approaches to teaching a skill. Below is a table containing a list of three critical approaches, namely task analysis, chaining, and video modeling.

Approaches	How They Work	Instances
Task Analysis	a. *The process of breaking a skill down into smaller steps.* b. *Teach each step individually until they are mastered and come together as a sequence called "chaining."* c. *Use visuals such as a checklist or pictures to aid in understanding the sequence of steps.* d. *Customize the steps into the smallest*	**Washing hands** a. *Turn on the faucet.* b. *Put hands underwater to get them wet.* c. *Put soap on hands.* d. *Scrub hands together for 20 seconds.* e. *Put hands underwater.* f. *Rinse.* g. *Turn water off.* h. *Dry hands.*

		action that is needed for each individual.*	
		*Take into consideration the age, skill level, and prior experience of the person. One person may be told to "turn on the faucet" and need only one step. Another person may need smaller steps: "Place your right hand on the faucet. Pull the handle up. Put the handle in the middle."	

Back Chaining		a. Uses a task analysis to teach a skill in reverse order.
		
		b. Back chaining sets
			Making a peanut butter and jelly sandwich
			
			   a. Parent:
			      i. Pick out a plate.
			      ii. Take a knife from the

the child up for success by completing the entire task.

c. Do all of the steps with the child watching or being prompted except the last step. Focus on teaching the last step.

d. Once the last step is mastered, move on to the second to last step, and so on.

iii. Get the peanut butter jar.

iv. Pick out the type of jelly.

v. Place the bread on the counter.

vi. Tear off a paper towel.

vii. Open the bread bag.

viii. Place two slices of bread on a plate.

ix. Open the peanut butter jar.

x. Dip a knife into the jar to get peanut butter.

xi. Use the knife to spread peanut butter on bread.

xii. Wipe off the knife with a

			xiii. *Open the jelly jar.*
			xiv. *Dip the knife into the jar to get jelly.*
			xv. *Use a knife to spread jelly on another slice of bread.*
			xvi. *Set down knife.*
		b.	*Child:*
			i. *Put both pieces of bread together.*
			ii. *Eat.*
Video Modeling	a.	*Video modeling is a teaching strategy that allows an individual to watch a video of a person doing a skill they*	

are trying to learn.

b. *This strategy works well for visual learners.*

c. *The person can pause the video after each step to give themselves time to do the action.*

d. *The video can be rewatched many times for skill acquisition.*

e. *Videos can be of the individual (video self-modeling), a family member, or an unknown person.*

Practice

One of the most effective ways to learn a skill is through constant practice. Here are some tips for getting the most out of the practice sessions with your teen:

a. Help them focus on one or two life skills at a time. Oversaturation can be counterproductive.

b. Engage your teen in chores that can be classified as being developmentally appropriate.

c. Take advantage of diverse environments to practice skills. This will help in oversimplifying the skill.

   i. For instance, money management skills should be taught at home, school, and a variety of stores and restaurants.

d. Engage the skills with different people at different times. This will help with further diversification.

   i. Request that family and friends help your child practice their newly acquired skills.

e. Volunteer in the community to work on job and executive functioning skills

Chapter 11

Life Skills—Safety Awareness

It is expected that you and your family would have acknowledged and given a number of talks on safety issues in the home by the time your child reaches adolescence and, to a large extent possible, have them under control. Simultaneously, newfangled concerns peculiar to adolescence arise; which lean toward experiences outside the home, such as at school, in the local community, and yonder, courtesy of the internet and social media.

Aside from the commencement of puberty and its accompanying changes, the teenage experience ranging from amplified importance of social life and interactive relationships to the longing for independence, privacy, and more adult responsibilities comes with a distinctive set of challenges and concerns.

As a parent, your most central role at this time is to care for your adolescent, be predominantly accustomed to their school environment, and continue to help them cultivate and practice safety awareness, alongside other life skills that they will take into adulthood. Stimulating independence is essential for youth and adults who have ASD, but there abound a lot of safety trepidations. As parents or guardians, it is quite a test to think ahead of all the dangers. Coming up with a safety plan and revising it once in a while is essential.

As children with ASD grow toward young adulthood, they may want to be involved and discover the community environment more individualistically. As a parent or guardian, it is your responsibility to ensure that you are giving your child the skills that they might need to be as safe as possible. Given that youth and adults with ASD may vary in their intellectual and developmental stages, there is the possibility of them lacking safety awareness and not fully grasping the concept of consequences for risky behaviors when they're out in the community. Being proactive and planning by methodically teaching them topics linked to safety can improve their safety when they're out in the community.

Here are a few areas that are worth considering when teaching safety skills to teens with ASD.

A. In the Community

If you get any indication that your child is deficient when it comes to safety awareness when they're in the community, then you might have to ponder teaching them and preparing them for the following types of circumstances:

- What to do if approached by a stranger.

- What to do if approached by one or more persons wanting their possessions.

- Best areas to walk. For instance, hanging around in peopled areas and shunning back alleys.

- What to do if grabbed by someone.

- How to use communal restrooms in a safe and socially acceptable way.

Exercise

Please answer the following questions:

1. *Have you had any conversations with your teen about safety awareness in the community?*

   Yes _____   *No* _____

2. *What are some of the dangers that loom in and around your neighborhood that your teen needs to be aware of?*

   _____
   _____
   _____
   _____
   _____
   _____

3. *Ask your teen if they have experienced anything in the community that gave them safety concerns.*

_____
_____
_____
_____
_____
_____

4. What other strategies would you teach your teen to further enhance their sense of safety?

_____
_____
_____
_____
_____
_____

B. Public Transportation

If your teen is ready to use public transportation, you might want to prepare them for the following circumstances that may occur:

- What to do if the teen missed their stop.

- How to deal with strangers who may approach them on the bus.

- What to do in the event that the bus doesn't arrive at their stop on time, or doesn't arrive at all.

- Review the bus routes the teen would be using. For instance, print out the map or schedule ahead of time.

- What to do if the teen loses their bus pass or bus tickets. For instance, always carry some spare change when going on a bus.

Exercise

Please answer the following questions:

1. *Have you had any conversations with your teen about public transportation safety?*

    Yes _____   *No* _____

2. *What are some of the dangers that loom in and around public transportation that your teen needs to be aware of?*

    _____
    _____
    _____
    _____
    _____
    _____

3. *Ask your teen if they have experienced anything while using public transportation that gave them safety concerns.*

    _____
    _____

_____
_____
_____
_____

4. *What other strategies would you teach your teen to further enhance their sense of safety while using public transportation?*

_____
_____
_____
_____
_____

C. Shopping in the Community

Here are a few things to teach your teen with ASD before they begin to go shopping in the community:

- In the event where stores do not allow customers to bring their backpacks or large bags into the store, parents have to teach the teen what to do if they come into this situation. Some individuals with ASD may not want to leave their belongings at the front counter.

- Teach the teen how to budget.

- What to do when approached by store security.

- Make sure the teen knows the rules of paying for items. They should not allow friends or others to persuade them into taking something from a store (shoplifting) without paying for it first.

Exercise

Please answer the following questions:

1. *Have you had any conversations with your teen about shopping in the community?*

    Yes _____   No _____

2. *What are some of the dangers that loom in and around shopping in the community that your teen needs to be aware of?*

    _____
    _____
    _____
    _____
    _____
    _____

3. *Ask your teen if they have experienced anything while shopping in the community that gave them safety concerns.*

    _____
    _____
    _____
    _____

4. What other strategies would you teach your teen to further enhance their sense of safety while shopping in the community?

_____
_____
_____
_____
_____

D. Law Enforcement

If your teen with ASD gets approached by a law enforcement officer, it is essential that they are aware of how to handle these situations:

- What to do when approached by the law enforcement officer. For instance, how to behave and where to keep hands.

- How to tell the law enforcement officer that they have autism.

- How to contact the police if they are in danger.

Exercise

Please answer the following questions:

1. Have you had any conversations with your teen about law enforcement?

    Yes _____   No _____

2. What are some of the dangers that loom in and around your community when it comes to law enforcement that your teen needs to be aware of?

    _____
    _____
    _____
    _____
    _____

    3. Ask your teen if they have experienced anything with law enforcement that gave them safety concerns.

    _____
    _____
    _____
    _____
    _____
    _____

4. *What other strategies would you teach your teen to further enhance their sense of safety while dealing with law enforcement officers?*

_____
_____
_____
_____
_____
_____
_____
_____

E. Internet Safety

If your teen with ASD is using the internet often, consider teaching them ways to improve their safety in these areas:

a. How to stay safe in chat rooms. For instance, do not give strangers personal information, do not share pictures of yourself with others, do not arrange to meet up with strangers online in person, and understand what a socially acceptable chat looks like.

b. How to keep passwords and online accounts protected. For instance, how to change your password intermittently, not share your passwords with others, and log out of accounts you are signed into when you are done.

Exercise

Please answer the following questions:

1. *Have you had any conversations with your teen about internet safety?*

    Yes _____   *No* _____

2. *What are some of the dangers that loom in and around your community when it comes to internet safety?*

_____
_____
_____
_____

3. Ask your teen if they have experienced anything online that gave them safety concerns.

_____
_____
_____
_____
_____

4. What other strategies would you teach your teen to further enhance their sense of safety online?

_____
_____
_____
_____
_____
_____

F. Money Management

It is essential that all parents teach their teens with ASD how to safely handle their money and bank cards. It is also important to note that some teens with ASD may need more teaching and guidance with handling money than others. Make sure to review and teach the following to improve their safety:

a. How to use debit and/or credit cards. It is imperative to instruct them never to give anyone their bank card or their bank card password.

b. How to be aware of surroundings when using ATMs alone or at night.

c. Teach them how to put away money into their wallet after using it. Teach them the appropriate amounts of cash to carry (large amounts of cash are not necessary).

G. Sexual Awareness and Autism Spectrum Disorder

Sex and sexuality are very challenging subjects for most parents to openly talk about, most especially with their wards. The nature of the subjects breeds apprehension and discomfort between the parents and their kids. But like everyone else, kids with ASD are bound to go through puberty and have desires or urges to be in a romantic relationship. This means that it is very important that parents teach their teenage kids with ASD about the topics associated with sex and sexuality to improve their safety.

Teens with ASD vary in their intellectual and developmental stages; this brings about a varied sense of awareness of sexual knowledge and safety amongst them. Some teens with ASD might not be conscious of their bodily changes that are taking place during puberty, privacy rules, or of the socially acceptable rules for romantic relationships.

Because of this, teens with ASD are a susceptible population who are at amplified risk for being sexually abused or exploited. It is helpful to prepare for and teach earlier rather than later the following topics to your teen with ASD:

- Educate your teen early on about the changes that their body is going to experience and what they should expect when in puberty.

- Educate your teen on the appropriate sexual behaviors they can engage in at home as opposed to out in the community.

- Educate your teen on inappropriate sexual behaviors they shouldn't participate in at home or in the community.

- Educate your teen on what sexual, physical, verbal, and emotional harassment is. For instance, what it may look like, what to do if they are being sexually harassed, and who to turn to if they think they are being sexually harassed.

- Explain suitable and respectful behaviors that people in a romantic relationship will engage in.

- Explain inappropriate and disrespectful behaviors that people in a romantic relationship should not engage in.

- Explain to them what a healthy romantic relationship looks like. For instance, how two individuals would feel about each other, how a relationship normally looks, the stages one normally goes through leading up to sex, and what sexual consent means.

- Teach your child about sex. For instance, what it is, the body parts of different genders, and the body parts involved in having sex.

- Explain healthy safe sex practices, such as using a condom or using birth control for females. Explain the results of not using safe sex practices.

Exercise

Please answer the following questions:

1. *Have you had any conversations with your teen about sex and sexuality?*

    Yes _____ *No* _____

2. *What are some of the dangers that loom in and around your community when it comes to sex and sexuality?*

_____
_____
_____
_____

3. Ask your teen if they have experienced anything about sex and sexuality that gave them safety concerns.

4. What other strategies would you teach your teen to further enhance their sense of safety when it comes to sex and sexuality?

Chapter 12

Life Skills—Self-Determination/Advocacy

Growing up, teenagers with ASD get used to things being done for them that their typical peers do themselves and that, in most cases, they ought to be able to do for themselves. From picking their clothes out in the morning to determining what classes to take and which extracurricular activities to be involved in, teens with ASD are always in the hands of helpers and advocates. However, all teenagers, even those who are very young or have limited language, can be taught to become self-advocates.

A. What Is Self-Advocacy?

Self-advocacy is having the right to make and express one's own life choices and decisions. Self-advocacy talks about a person's ability to excellently communicate, express, negotiate, or assert their interests, desires, needs, and rights. It comprises making informed choices and taking responsibility for those decisions. Various studies establish a clear connection between teaching children self-advocacy skills and their ability to attain happiness and become well-functioning adults. For some people, self-advocacy is the one thing that keeps their social life buoyant; making a normal life is possible. For others, no one will know what they can or can't do, or what they truly desire without the ability to self-advocate.

Self-advocacy includes these modules:

- Encouraging the use of language that is inclusive, respectful, and person-first

- Knowing what services, modifications, and accommodations you need and being able to demand them

- Knowing whom to ask and where to go to get assistance and support

- Appreciating and expressing one's strengths, talents, and interests

- Being able to formulate personal goals and choose necessary paths to achieve those goals

- Having the ability to make choices

B. How Can You Help Teenagers with Autism Spectrum Disorder Learn to Self-Advocate?

Include students in the individualized education program process.

- The special education law (IDEA 2004) says that all students must be included to the best of their ability.

- Use simple language or even pictures to help students with ASD understand their strengths and areas of need.

- Start to include children at an early age at their meetings, even if it is just introductions for a few minutes at first. You can provide incentives such as a favorite food at the meeting; this can help sustain their interest.

- When dealing with the students, they should be spoken to, not about.

- Older students can prepare and share a PowerPoint discussing their IEP—goals, accommodations, present levels of performance—in their own words (and pictures).

Give children the freedom to make choices.

- Use penchant and reinforcer surveys to decide what types of rewards and activities a child would like.

- Starting from an early age, present a child with choices: "Which do you want to do first: your homework or reading?"

- Let them learn that they have the right to say "no" so that they can say it to appeals that are irrational or precarious.

- Role-play scenarios that involve making a choice. For instance, if you are in a department store shopping, ask your child which person they would go to for help if they couldn't find you. You can role-play scenarios across several settings.

Teach self-advocacy skills.

- Use a checklist to ascertain which skills a teen already has and which they need to learn.

- Teens should know about their disability and how and when to disclose their needs to others.

- Teach children to begin taking a role in planning their activities, such as using a calendar.

- Encourage children to try to do activities that they can do on their own as independently as possible.

Here are suggestions on teaching your teen when and how to express what they need:

C. Educate the Teen on the Difference between Needs and Preferences

Before a teen can self-advocate for what they need, they first have to be taught the difference between things they absolutely must have and things they would like to have. The teen might need clarification on the importance of attending to their needs rather than simply asking for whatever they want. This practice has to begin very early in the teen's life; this way, they get used to not having their way and thereby not making a mess of anything when they are denied their requests. Once the teen can adequately separate between needs and wants, their request would always be taken seriously.

Exercise

- *Make out time to have a chat with your teen about needs and preferences.*
- *Explain to the teen the difference between having a need and having a preference.*
- *Use instances that the teen can relate to. You can also use instances that involve you; this will help build the kid's confidence, and they will see you as a role model.*
- *Allow the teen to ask questions, and attempt to clarify them.*

Take note of the various responses of the teen at each stage and with each instruction.

Important notes:

_____
_____
_____
_____
_____
_____
_____
_____
_____

D. Have Teens Write a Note to Their Teachers

You can encourage your teen to draft out a letter to each of their teachers. The letter should clearly outline who they are, what they like and dislike, what stresses them out, and what they need to succeed. This isn't only a great self-awareness exercise for your teen but also a great resource for teachers to have right away. In addition, it can give teachers a quick summary of the student before they've had time to sit down and read an entire IEP. You can also encourage the teen to give the notes to the teachers themself before the school year begins. It is clear that a lot of teachers will appreciate this gesture from your teen as it is tantamount to the student coming to the teachers and telling them what exactly they need to be successful.

Exercise

- *Make out time to have a chat with your teen about drafting a note for their teachers.*

- *Explain to the teen the impact that such a note would have on the teachers and their confidence.*

- *Allow the teen to ask questions, and attempt to clarify them.*

- *Help the teen in formulating a template for the letters.*

> Take note of the various responses of the teen at each stage and with each instruction.

Important notes:

_____
_____
_____
_____
_____
_____
_____
_____
_____

E. Include the Child in Individualized Education Program Meetings

Attending IEP meetings, either in full or in part, would help the teen understand how things work and why they get certain services or accommodations, but not others. It also gives room for the teen to voice out their concerns about situations that may be challenging for them. It should be noted that not every child has the language skills to express their needs in such meetings; however, even a simple yes and no, verbally, via gestures, or with an assistive communication device could be used, thereby boosting the teen's self-esteem.

Exercise

- *Make out time to have a chat with your teen about attending IEP meetings.*

- *Explain to the teen the impact that attending such a meeting would have on them and the team members.*

- *Allow the teen to ask questions, and attempt to clarify them.*

Take note of the various responses of the teen at each stage and with each instruction.

Important notes:
_____
_____
_____
_____
_____
_____
_____
_____
_____
_____

F. Encourage the Teen to Share Information with the Right People

The teen needs to know whom they can go to if they have a challenge. Parents ought to discuss with their teens when and with whom they can share their needs or disclose their diagnosis. If not, they might start sharing with other students, unnecessarily, giving bullies room to use the information against them.

Exercise

- *Make out time to have a chat with your teen about sharing sensitive and private information*

- *Explain to the teen the impact that such an action can have on their emotional and social well-being.*

- *Allow the teen to ask questions, and attempt to clarify them.*

- *Compile a list of important people that the teen might share sensitive information with: they may include a close friend, a teacher, the school's counselor, and so on.*

Take note of the various responses of the teen at each stage and with each instruction.

Important notes:
_____
_____
_____
_____
_____
_____
_____
_____
_____
_____

Chapter 13

Life Skills—The Seven Essential Life Skills for Success in Teenagers with Autism

A. Executive Functioning Skills

These are managerial abilities that are required to plan the day, break down a task, create a to-do list, and plan for chores, outings, and so on. Building this skill is not a one-off exercise at all; it will be an ongoing process, as it is a challenging feat for most teens with ASD. But with a lot of care and practice, your teen would prevail. Soon, they will have the ability to manage their surroundings to the point of being effective.

It is important to take them one step after the other and one day at a time. This skill is delicate and hard to master, especially for teens with autism who possess varying levels of intellectual capacity and development. Each step should be accompanied by parental praise and encouragement.

B. Practical Living Skills

These skills incorporate the art of seeking out information (from the internet, books, newspapers, and so on), learning money management (budgeting, bank accounts, credit cards, making change), exploring travels (reading a map, using transportation, planning and going on a trip), choosing a fashion sense (care, laundering, organizing, makeup), home management (garbage day, housecleaning, doing dishes), home economics, and shopping.

One of the best ways to get your teen to imbibe these skills is by involving them in your daily routine, rather than doing everything for them. Furthermore, the earlier they are included in activities such as cooking, cleaning, and laundry, the longer they have to develop comfort and routines in these key areas. Another way to teach your kids these vital skills is to expose them to groups that share common interests in any of the above skills. This will help the teen loosen up and learn faster.

C. Personal Care

This entails personal daily hygiene, exercise, nutrition, dealing with an illness such as a cold, and coping with stress. You can fashion out and practice relaxation routines, make task breakdown lists for showering, toileting, or toothbrushing. Personal care can be a challenge for teens with ASD to learn; this is not only because do they not possess the intellectual capacity to uphold so many of these activities but also because they have been taken care of their entire life, with others handling their care. Furthermore, for some, the activities are extremely irritating to them. For instance, some teens with autism might hate water; others may hate the taste of toothpaste, and so on. The parent can do a number of things to help encourage the teen to step up their personal life.

D. Job Skills

Your teen needs to be taught how people generally look for jobs, create resumes, get work experience, and become good employees. A good place to begin to gain job experience may be via volunteer work. So if the parents volunteer for an organization, it would be smart to take the teen along too to gain some experience. Other volunteer avenues to try are through churches, sports clubs, guides or scouts, museums, parks and recreation, the library—the list is endless. Try to find a good fit with the teen's interests.

E. Personal Safety

This is an important but tough topic to teach. Many teens with ASD will learn rules like don't talk to strangers, but will not know when to break those rules if needed. Under stress, some teens with autism lose their ability to speak. So, you can begin by making handy cards for the teen to carry around with a few statements on them for those stressful moments when it can be hard to gather one's thoughts. You should also teach them about risks and how to avoid dangerous situations. For instance, one rule may be not to use public transportation after dark if in a big city. Another may be not to do favors for an unfamiliar person.

F. People Skills

Typically, this would fall under the topic of social skills; however, people skills are extremely important for life if the teen is to form a healthy friendship, interactions, and romance in the future. Areas that need to be groomed are working in a group, making friends, asking for help, dealing with family relationships, communicating over the phone, conversation, and so on. Even though social rules and etiquette can be taught if the child is high functioning enough, you can also consider teaching flexibility in thinking and perspective-taking.

The attainment of life skills is an ongoing process. All skills take time to be obtained and become fluent with. It is best to begin working on all of these skills while the child still lives at home. Ensure that your teen's school has a life skills program, as this should be a fundamental part of every teen's education.

Exercise

1. *From the above listings in this chapter, which of the aforementioned categories would you say is lacking in your teen and why?*

   _____
   _____
   _____
   _____
   _____

2. *In which of the aforementioned categories has your teen largely excelled?*

   _____
   _____
   _____

3. What modalities do you intend to put in place to help your teen improve in the aforementioned life skills?

Chapter 14

Life Skills—Ten Ways to Build Your Teen's Independence

A. Strengthen Communication

In the event that your teen still struggles with spoken language, a critical step for growing independence is by strengthening their ability to communicate. This can be done by building and making tools available to aid in expression of preferences, desires, and feelings. You can ponder on whether to introduce Alternative/Augmentative Communication (AAC) and visual supports. Common types of AAC include picture exchange communication systems (PECS), speech output devices (such as DynaVox, iPad, etc.).

Exercise

- *Practice healthy communication with your teen. This can be done by creating a favorable atmosphere for trust and openness.*

- *Practice listening to your teen. Do not make every occasion about teaching.*

- *Get help when you need it. It isn't always easy to teach the art of communication all by yourself*

B. Introduce a Visual Calendar

Employing the use of a visual schedule with your teen can assist in the transition from activity to activity with less stimulation. Appraise each item on the calendar with your teen and then remind them to check the calendar before every transition. As time passes, they will be able to complete these tasks with increased independence, practice decision-making, and pursue the activities that interest them.

Exercise

- *It is important to engage your teen in planning the calendar.*

- *Do not be overly sensitive or extreme. Take each day at a time.*

- *Give room for do-overs. Teenagers will always come short; just make sure they keep moving.*

C. Teach Your Child to Ask for a Break

It is important for your teen to have a way of requesting a break. If your teen uses a communicator device, you can add in a "Break" button. Furthermore, you can place a picture in the teen's PECS book, and so on. Also, find an area that is quiet where your teen can go when feeling astounded. On the other hand, contemplate offering headphones or other tools to aid in regulating sensory inputs. Even though it may look like a simple thing, knowing how to ask for a break can allow your teen to reclaim control over their mind and environment.

Exercise

- *Talk to your teen about the possibility of needing a break. Make them realize that it is all right to ask for one.*

- *You can put up a routine for breaks. This can help in triggering your teen to consider such a possibility.*

- *Teach your teen responsibility. They are not expected to abuse the right to ask for breaks.*

D. Work on Household Chores

Once you can have your kids complete their household chores, they will learn a great deal of responsibility. Getting them involved in family routines will also help impart useful skills to take with them as they get older. If you think your teen may have trouble appreciating how to complete a whole chore, you can ponder on using task analysis. This is a technique that involves breaking down large tasks into smaller steps. Be sure to model the steps yourself or provide prompts if your child has trouble at first.

Exercise

- *Be the first example for your teen. Seeing someone they love and respect doing what is expected will always trigger them to emulation.*

- *Start by delegating little responsibilities first before giving them bigger ones.*

- *You can help them with as much supervision as they would require; then gradually pull away to help them establish self-confidence in their actions.*

E. Practice Money Skills

Learning how to use money is a very essential skill that can aid your teen in becoming independent when they're out and about in the community. No matter what abilities your teen currently showcases, there are ways that they can begin to learn money skills. At school, consider adding money skills to your teen's IEP and when you are with your child in a store or supermarket, allow them to hand over the money to the cashier. Step by step, you can teach each part of this process. Your child can then begin using these skills in different settings in the community.

Exercise

- *Introduce your child to rudimentary bookkeeping. Let them account for all their incomes and expenditures.*

- *Help them plan their spending; guide them in choosing what to buy and how to spend.*

- *Tie them to a budget, and keep the cap. Don't be tempted to give them more if they squander what was within their planned budget.*

F. Teach Community Safety Skills

Safety is a big disquiet for many families, particularly as teenagers become more independent. You can teach and practice travel training including pedestrian safety, identifying signs and other significant safety markers, and becoming familiar with public transportation. Consider having your teen carry an ID card which can be very helpful in providing their name, a brief explanation of their diagnosis, and a contact person.

Exercise

- *Discuss with your teen the realities of safety.*

- *Role-play with your child on how to behave and act around various situations that warrant concern for safety.*

- *Encourage your child to be law-abiding, and teach them how to call on law enforcement.*

G. Build Leisure Skills

The ability to engage in independent leisure and recreation is a skill that will help your teen well throughout their lives. A lot of teens with autism have special interests in one or two topics; leisure can aid in translating those interests into age-appropriate recreational activities. There are a lot of resource guides online that contain activities that your teen can get involved in within your community; including team sports, swim lessons, martial arts, music groups, and more.

Exercise

- *Take time out to enjoy leisure with your teen.*

- *Ensure to not mix business with pleasure. Let the teen see from your actions that leisure is time to relax and not engage in work while at it.*

- *Help your teen discover their most preferred way of relaxing.*

H. Teach Self-Care during Adolescence

You can bring self-care activities into your teen's routine. Brushing teeth, combing hair, and other activities of daily living (ADLs) are imperative life skills, and bringing them in as early as you possibly can lets your teen master them down the line. Ensure that you include these things in your child's schedule so they can get used to having them as part of the daily routine.

Also, your teen with ASD is bound to experience many changes as they enter adolescence and beginning puberty. This means that this is an essential time to introduce many hygiene and self-care skills. Getting your teens into the habit of self-care will place them on the road to success and allow them to become much more independent as they approach adulthood. Visual aids can be useful in helping them complete their hygiene routine each day. Contemplate making a checklist of activities to aid your teen in keeping track of what to do, and post it in the bathroom. This can include items such as showering, washing face, putting on deodorant, and brushing hair.

To stay structured, you can put together a hygiene "kit" to keep everything your teen needs in one place.

Exercise

- *Be the first example for your teen. They learn better when lessons are personified by people they love and respect.*

- *Set up multiple ways of reminding and reinforcing the need for self-care.*

- *Discuss self-care in daily conversations to familiarize the teen with them.*

- *When your teen misses a routine like forgetting to brush in the morning, have them do it immediately.*

I. Work on Vocational Skills

Beginning from age fourteen, your teen should have vocational skills included in their IEP as a part of an adapted transition plan. Make a list of their strengths, skills, and interests, and use them to guide the type of vocational activities that are included as goals. Consider all the ways up to this point that you have been nurturing your teen's independence: communication abilities, self-care, interests, and activities, and goals for the future.

Exercise

- *Talk to your teen about the importance of vocational skills.*

- *Introduce your teen to various vocational organizations. This will help them with choosing which to pursue.*

- *Listen to your teen. They may have certain concerns or reservations that need to be addressed.*

Chapter 15

Life Skills—Personal Finance

Money management skills are important if you desire to help your teen become more independent as they grow up. However, there is no fairytale timeline as to when your teen or an adult with autism may learn all of these money management skills successfully. It will all come over time, as each child is unique to when they may learn various skills.

A fresh study projected to shed light on exactly this issue has pointed out that when teenagers and young adults with autism enter adulthood and outgrow many of the services intended to aid them, they frequently are nervous about how to handle new adult responsibilities like paying bills and filing taxes. These findings focus on the importance of slotting financial management into early education to empower young adults with autism.

A. Tips to Help with Money Management through Daily Activities

Below are a few tips to help your teen with money management. Indicate the level of commitment you have put in each one.

		Always	Sometimes	Never
1.	I allow my teen to pay for items at the store.			
2.	I give my teen an allowance and save up for items to buy at the store.			
3.	I take my teen to the bank with me and discuss how the bank works.			
4.	I helped my teen open up a savings or a checking account.			
5.	I have my teen list out their wants and needs.			
6.	I talk about money habits with my teen, such as helping them set up a budget.			
7.	My teen has a job; we talk about their paycheck, and I help them understand their benefits and taxes.			
8.	We find coupons and special deals on products from newspaper ads and grocery ads.			
9.	I use apps and online resources to aid my teen in learning money skills.			

10.	I help my teen in planning their monthly income and expenses.			
11.	I look up the prices of items (wants and needs) that my teens want to get to figure out if they have enough money or what they will need to earn.			
12.	I give my teen workbooks to learn about money skills.			
13.	I encourage my teen to practice paying with cash.			
14.	I take my teen to the grocery store. We find items, and I show them the different prices of the same item. I also help them learn which items are the best deals or bring along coupons and have them find the items they need to use the coupons.			
15.	I teach my teen to save their receipts and practice reviewing the purchases so as to keep track of their spending.			
16.	I encourage my teen to go through some common monthly bills such as housing and food, utilities so that they can get			

	an idea of how much those items cost. I talk to them about ways by which they can pay those bills either online or by check in the mail.			

Exercise

1. Discuss with your teen how you can improve on the above-listed money management skills.

2. Discuss any other money habits that you may feel can help improve their skills

3. Discuss money practices that must be dropped to attain improved money management skills.

B. Transportation

Transportation involves the practice of moving between locations and also necessitates that the person would transition on and off the transportation device. The use of transportation is an indispensable skill without which a person could not self-sufficiently function throughout the day or access essential services such as education, employment, conveniences, and social events. Here, we will discuss transitional approaches used in the support of adolescent with autism that experience difficulties linked to their educational placement and transportation.

Stress, predominantly arising from changes that were unexpected on the transport timetables can lead to teens with autism trying to avoid public transport altogether, greatly reducing excitement or enthusiasm for traveling away from home. For teens with autism, satisfactory transportation can offer freedom and independence by increasing mobility.

C. Public Transport Tips that are Autism Friendly

Use a sketch or sign.

The frequent use of visual aids can assist teens with autism. This could be drafted as scripts or vividly drawn pictures describing every step required to use public transport and what to do if the bus is late. You can also teach kindness using scripts, in addition to offering a seat to elderly/pregnant women/other passengers, and teaching coping approaches if the teen's most preferred seat or driver is taken or not there, respectively. Scripts and visuals are invaluable for managing emotions when the bus is missed or other unforeseen events occur. Other things that can be represented as signs, scripts, or sketches include forecasting alternate routes and directions on how to check timetables.

Cake out noise.

Your teen can wear headphones to lessen background noise and play soothing music through them. Some travelers with autism use headphones as a generally acceptable way of signaling that they do not wish to engage in any conversation.

Carry a familiar object.

Your teen can tag along with a favorite book, phone, toy, a piece of cloth, or something with a familiar scent or texture. Favorite scents on a bandanna can assist with shunning unpleasant smells. This can aid in comforting and distracting, reducing anxiety, and avoiding a sensory overload.

Travel at quiet times whenever possible.

Achieving this might be next to impossible in some climes, but escaping rush hours can lessen the stress of public transport. If the train or bus is full, have approaches to cope with waiting for the next one, which may be less crowded. Your teen might prefer sitting next to an exit, but you have to make sure that there are strategies such as a script or visual support for selecting a different seat if this seat is not available.

Plan and practice making the trips and learn strategies to cope with change.

The occasional exploration of diverse routes will aid in reducing anxiety. Always have a backup plan for all the possible unforeseen changes, including changed drivers, changed routes, roadblocks, and breakdowns.

Below are a few tips to help your teen with transportation. Indicate the level of commitment you have put in each one.

		Always	Sometimes	Never
1.	My teen uses a sketch or sign.			
2.	My teen uses earphone to cake out the noise.			
3.	My teen carries familiar objects.			
4.	My teen travels at quiet times whenever possible.			
5.	I plan and practice making the trips with my teen.			

Exercise

- *Discuss with your teen how you can improve on the above-listed transport skills.*

- *Discuss any other transport habits that you may feel can help improve their skills.*

- *Discuss transport practices that must be dropped to attain improved money management skills.*

Chapter 16

Life Skills—Teaching Adolescents with Autism to Drive

For adolescents with autism and their families, it can be challenging to get the backing they need to securely circumnavigate the learning-to-drive process or to trail other ways of becoming independently mobile.

A recently published research that scrutinized the process and experience of driving instructors who offer behind-the-wheel training particularly to adolescents and young adults with autism indicate that two in three high-functioning adolescents with autism of legal driving age are either presently driving or plan to drive. Furthermore, the majority of adolescents with autism who got a learner's permit went on to become fully licensed, which is suggestive of the fact that families make the decision to drive before the permit stage, not during it.

This research further reveals a number of common themes which arose from interviews:

- The support of parents of adolescents with autism is critical for their teens when it comes to making the choice to drive and engage the learning-to-drive process. Professional expert driving instructors see parents as fundamental associates in supporting their efforts to teach driving skills and promote independence.

- The support and highlighting of teen's independence by their parents before beginning the learning-to-drive process are critical. The driving instructors encourage parents to help their adolescents with autism cultivate life skills, such as mowing the lawn, cooking, and taking public transportation. These skills are critical in increasing independence and making a successful transition to adulthood.

- Best practices to notify valuation and instructional methods are greatly needed. Presently, there are no standardized valuation methods or instructional strategies to follow. This need for practice recommendations may be particularly important for nonspecialized instructors who are providing lessons to teens with autism without the benefit of additional training or access to specialized resources. However, driving instructors also are aware that specific approaches will unavoidably be tailored to meet the individual and unique needs of each adolescent driver with autism.

D. Resources for Families

Apart from encouraging development and mastery of independent living skills, here are a few suggestions for families to improve driver training:

- Don't do it yourself; seek help from Vocational Rehabilitation Services. Even though this might come at a price, it is worth it, as it will be financial support for instruction. Information is available from the Rehabilitation Services Administration.

- You can do the critical acts of helping the child formulate independent life skills in various areas such as personal hygiene, health, food preparation, housekeeping, and transportation.

- You can offer ample parent-supervised driving instruction in collaboration with professional driving instructors. The Driving Plan Practice Guide recommends evidence-based instruction in six driving environments, at night, and in harsh weather.

- Access individualization of instruction designed to meets the needs of peculiar learner drivers where available. Certified Driver Rehabilitation Specialists or Occupational Therapists (OTs) can deliver dedicated training and recommendations for adolescent drivers with autism.

Exercise

- *Discuss with your teen about the possibility of them learning to drive.*

- *Listen to their fears and concerns.*

- *Encourage them to grow past their reservations, and assure them of all the support that they would need to learn.*

- *Visit the driving institute for learning for some sightseeing. This might help them see things differently if they are still skeptical.*

- *Introduce them to driving professionals who may encourage them to learn.*

Chapter 17

Life Skills—Career Path and Employment

As kids with autism grow to become teenagers, parents ask the critical question of whether or not they would be able to get a job, whether or not they will be able to get into college, or how best they can help their kids prepare to get there. The best responses to these concerns are partly contingent on where a child falls on the autism spectrum. Nevertheless, with the right training and planning aimed at their capabilities, teens can find their path to a great job—and in many cases go on to college as well. Autism therapists have outlined methods that parents can use to prepare their wards with autism for these outside-the-home mileposts on their journey as a teen growing into early adulthood.

A. Plan at a Young Age

Once your child gets introduced to the ideas of vocations and career paths early in life, they are likely to discover and develop their exact interests sooner rather than later. Teens with autism, as with any child growing up, often try to imagine what they want to be when they grow up, and the answer to their mental questions isn't always clear. This is why they require a lot of time and space to try out a few, changing their minds to activities they uniquely enjoy as they go on.

Typically, vocation training for a child with autism begins around age fourteen. Beginning this kind of training and education early affords the teen ample time required to grow real-world skills that will aid them later in college or a job. In addition, such early actions and education focus unambiguously on cultivating the many skills and conducts necessary at work or school.

B. Capabilities-based Job Options

Real-life work experiences for your teen come with unique personal benefits that cannot be overstated. By holding down a part-time job, your teen gets the chance to see what work life is really like when parental supervision isn't anywhere nearby. Generally, autism programs assist teens with aspiring for one of three levels of job placement, namely:

- *Adult activity centers*: These centers offer job training skills expansion for lower-functioning individuals in an organized, thoughtful environment.

- *Supported employment*: It is getting increasingly common to have built-in support systems such as job coaches in agencies or offices today. This is best for individuals who are experts at their jobs but aren't necessarily independent.

- *Competitive employment*: This encompasses definite independent jobs for individuals. Holding down this job would necessitate the responsibility of transportation to and from work and day-to-day work activities.

C. Hard Skills and Soft Skills

For people with autism, hard and soft skills are assimilated behaviors that can take time and effort to attain, unlike individuals without autism, who find it much easier to learn. This is why it is imperative for parents to think outside the box when handling their kids with autism. This would mean incorporating life and social skills at very early stages in life to ready their teens for the future.

Vocational training imparts an assortment of hard skills necessary for performing job-specific responsibilities, such as activity-based tasks like how to file records, make pizza boxes, organize inventory, or prepare food. Others are transactional skills such as how to log data, work with money, read a calendar, or similar work-related tasks.

Furthermore, accompanying hard skills should be an assortment of the right soft skills as well. For teens with autism, situations at an archetypal job may be much more of an erudite effort. So the soft skill may teach the teen how to practice safety skills, when to ask for a break or vacation day, seek assistance from a supervisor, or how to resolve a conflict with a coworker.

D. Parent Involvement at Every Level

Observing your teen at work can give you a sense of what the teen is doing well; on the other hand, it also offers ways to underpin positive behavior at home. Your role as a parent can also make a big impression beyond just witnessing and underpinning. For instance, if your teen appears to be ready for competitive employment, you can explore your network for potential jobs. If they're good at filing or bookkeeping, ask if local stores or businesses have part-time job vacancies. If they love working outdoors, a construction agency might be a good fit. If your teen has communication issues, customized employment might be more appropriate. Ask your transition team if they know of agencies with vacations.

E. Considering College as an Option

A lot of high-functioning teens do well in a controlled academic environment such as college. And a lot of colleges and universities offer support services for older children or young adults with autism. For instance, some offer special floors in dorms with supportive resident advisers or academic coaches who appreciate and can work with their inimitable needs. A teen that shines in school may still face difficulties in the new, social, and occasionally frightening world of college.

A lot of the same vocational training values can also relate to the college prep process as your teen attempts to become more independent as a young adult. To assist in preparing them for college, it's also best to aid them in developing social and communications skills for their new environment. You should explore teaching skills related to self-care, goal-setting, techniques to handle multitasking, and learning how to ask for help when things get to be challenging for them.

Below are a few tips to help your teen with career path choices. Indicate the level of commitment you have put in each one.

		Always	Sometimes	Never
1.	I began planning for my teen at a young age.			
2.	I have taught my teen along with capabilities-based job options for better placement.			
3.	I teach my teen both hard skills and soft skills.			
4.	I am extremely involved at every level of my teen's life.			
5.	I have been preparing my teen for college.			

Exercise

- *Discuss with your teen on vocation and choosing career paths.*

- *Discuss any fears and concerns that your teen might have about vocations and career paths in general or in particular.*

- *Reassure them of your total commitment to their achieving their dreams.*

- *Discuss the possibilities of going to college.*

Chapter 18

Life Skills—Leisure/Recreation

We all know that leisure activities are an important part of life. Our general well-being is greatly upsurged whenever we engage in activities that are fun, enjoyable, and stimulating; this also contributes to our happiness and satisfaction in life. Whether we engage in leisure activities alone or in a group, at home or out in the community, we are bound to reap the benefits.

For kids with ASD, developing leisure interests and skills can be a bit more puzzling, as such skills are often not learned through simulations or unceremonious observation of others. Their interests are advanced in their way, as skills learned through one activity may not be generalized to another.

A. Why is Developing Leisure Skills Important?
- Baffling behaviors generally lessen in intensity whenever an individual takes part in individually satiating leisure activities. The aptitude to charm oneself can lessen apprehension for the individual both at home and in the community.

- Leisure skills and interests can provide social benefits, in that they increase bonding between individuals who share the same passion. Such activities bring a group of people together, who share an interest and like to talk about it. This level of exposure to a wide variety of activities and experiences widens interests. Nevertheless, interests are bound to change over time; this means that it is important to keep getting more experiences for growth and development.

B. Qualities that Make Leisure Materials and Activities More Effective

The following unambiguous qualities can make leisure activities more communicative and effective, bearing in mind that everyone has personal preferences.

Comprehensible.

Appreciating the purpose and the wherewithal of activity can sometimes be difficult for a teen with ASD. Here are a few tips on making things more comprehensible:

- Rules should be clear and fixed.
- Have well-established beginnings and endings.
- Each activity should be predictable or repetitive.
- All acts should be visually clear and well represented.
- Each activity should have nominal verbal instruction.

- Each activity should be well structured.

Active.

The development of the gross motor skills of young kids has to involve activities such as climbing, running, and jumping. In addition, rhythmic activities such as swinging or swimming are also good choices. No matter the age, individuals need physical activity that aids in reducing stress, growing muscles, and increasing flexibility and balance. Systematic exercise can also back an improved night's rest.

Visual-spatial.

It is extremely motivating for kids when they engage in activities that involve repetitive manipulation of objects, putting things in order, or fitting objects into spaces. There are lots of toys and games that provide these qualities, such as puzzles.

Reactive.

Sensory feedbacks are largely reinforced through reactive materials. These are generally lights, sounds, movement, and tactile sensation. Some leisure activities that provide such feedback are electronic and computer games, even though it can be a tussle to limit time on tech devices. Adding in music can spice up the activities as well.

Comfortable.

You can promote the comfort of each game by ensuring the following:

- You can dare without being overstimulating.

- You can make every activity fit in with the individual's ability levels.

- You can put a cap as regards the demands for multifaceted social interaction.

- You can give room for a sense of control or mastery.

Using the table below, analyze some of the games or activities you do with your teen. The idea is to determine if they meet the abovementioned criteria.

	Activity/game	*Comprehensible* >∨∧	*Active* >∨∧	*Visual-Spatial* >>∧	*Reactive* >∨∧	*Comfortable* >∨∧
Ex	We play board games.					
1						
2						

3										
4										
5										

C. How Can I Keep My Child Engaged after School?

Independent leisure skills.

Independent leisure skills are activities that your teen can revert to doing whenever they have some downtime. Activities can range from solving puzzle books and reading a book to drawing in a notebook. These activities are dense and can be very handy. Your teen will be able to keep themselves busy while waiting at a dentist's office, during a religious event, or at home while you are doing something important.

You can commence teaching independent leisure skills by creating a schedule and teaching your teen how to use it. You can also propose a rotational list of activities, homework, exercise, and chores with breaks scattered all the way through, and review it together with your teen daily until they become acquainted with it. You should also progressively dwindle out your oral prompts until they are able to complete the schedule independently.

You may choose to suggest a selection of activities to build up self-determination skills by saying, "Do you want to draw a picture OR work on a crossword puzzle?"

Fun constructive activities.

You can choose to engage your teen in activities that offer a model to follow, like a photo or list of steps. For instance, activities with easy-to-follow steps such as completing a Lego set, sticker books, Klutz books, and tangram puzzles. Also, crossword puzzles and word searches have a set list of items or words to find. Because step-by-step directions are built into the recipes, cooking and baking can be considered as good choices for an activity. Also, younger kids can help you complete a recipe by stirring, pouring in premeasured ingredients, or decorating a cake or cookies. Recipes help with math skills, fine motor skills, and life skills, especially for older children.

Homework.

It is important for kids to do their homework assignments, as it would help with improving their focus and flexibility. Choose a suitable time for your teen to complete their homework, and ensure that they stick to that time every day, as best you can. Also, it is important to know that after a long school day, some kids may need to decompress, and so taking walks or other physical activities would help. For others, they may enjoy a fun activity for a short period before attempting their homework assignments. Still others may prefer to do their homework right away, while still in school mode. You as a parent would need to experiment to realize which works best for your teen.

Furthermore, you can take the steps ahead by making a list of all assignments to be worked on and tracking how much time each will take. Finally, you can check off each assignment when completed. Once homework time begins to run, you can offer simple rewards like a drink of water, a piece of gum, or even doing jumping jacks; this will keep the kid on track. Another innovation would be the use of a Time Timer. This will give your teen an idea of how much time is left until the next break. Or simply proposing a break after completing a few assignments could keep them focused.

Chores.

Slotting in chores into your teen's after-school routine will teach them responsibility and self-help skills for the future. To begin, select chores that your teen enjoys or can be successful at right away. This initial sense of accomplishment at the very beginning will greatly improve their self-esteem. You can then go on to add to the chore list gradually, remembering to be patient with any inadequacies at the beginning.

Ensure that you give age-appropriate chores to your teen. There is countless remuneration for children with autism to do chores around the house.

Social activities.

Avail your teen the chance to work on social skills, be it a one-on-one activity with a peer or a group activity. Schools regularly propose improvement activities on school grounds that begin right after school. These are frequently very reasonably priced and can be a great way to include your teen in fun activities. City recreation departments are also good resources.

Another option is one-on-one playdates with friends. This can greatly work on social skills in the comfort of your own home. Also, formulating a visual timetable for the playdates will aid your teen in preparing for the length of time a friend will be visiting, as well as cope with the hopes of what they will be expecting. Use social stories before the playdate to review expected behaviors, proper manners, and other hypothetically problematic situations. You can also preteach games or play scenarios. While at the playdate, encourage turn-taking and interactions.

Games.
Engage your teen with games that help kids with autism work on social skills as well as fine motor skills, learning numbers and colors, or taking turns. Computer games are known to work on not just school-related skills but social and life skills also.

Volunteer openings.
Volunteering can be a great way to develop social skills, change over into their community, and grow relationships. Numerous establishments offer volunteering and job training opportunities. You can engage the use of visual schedules and supports to craft out a schedule for after-school time, just as you would for the morning or bedtime routines. The routine must be as similar as

possible, capturing regular activities and chores around any after-school activities. If need be, make a different schedule for each weekday.

Using visual supports to craft out the schedule will help in easy articulation of the routine and would make it easier to follow. Also, think about incorporating brain breaks during activities that necessitate devoted attention, like homework or reading.

You can employ the use of reward systems, as they are vital tools in assisting your teen. You can use rewards when they complete an apportioned chore or to encourage homework completion. Such rewards do not have to be spendthrift, and they should serve as distractions from the task at hand, such as watching TV or video games. You can use stickers or other low-cost collectible items like pencils or gum as rewards.

Chapter Nineteen: Life Skills—Home Living Skills

Practical life skills are essential for all individuals in learning and developing as they get older to learn to be more independent with their everyday lives. It can feel overpowering when you think about all the various areas of life skills you have to teach and that someone has to try to learn.

Below, you will find a large list of life skills you can help teach. Going through them will help you grasp their enormity and importance to your teen's mental, emotional, and physical growth.

E. Self-Care Skills

Dressing	Personal Hygiene	Kitchen Skills
<ul><li>*Taking shirt on and off*</li><li>*Taking pants on and off*</li><li>*Taking underwear on and off*</li><li>*Taking bra on and off*</li><li>*Taking socks*</li></ul>	<ul><li>Using the Toilet</li><li>Washing hands</li><li>Taking shower</li><li>Taking bath</li><li>Brushing hair</li><li>Brushing teeth</li></ul>	<ul><li>Making a sandwich</li><li>Getting a snack from the fridge or cupboard</li><li>Getting a bowl of cereal to eat</li><li>Making toast</li><li>Pouring self a drink (milk, water, or juice)</li><li>Reheating a</li></ul>

on and off • Taking shoes on and off • Tying shoes • Completing buttons and zippers on clothing • Tying a tie • Picking out appropriate clothes for the day/weather • Taking shirt on and off • • Taking pants on and off • Taking underwear on and off	• • Washing face • Flossing • • Shaving face • Shaving legs • • Handling menstrual cycle cleanliness • Applying makeup	meal in the microwave • Packing lunch for school • Following a basic recipe • • Using the toaster • Using the oven to make a meal • • Packing leftovers from dinner • • Reading food labels • Learning knife safety skills • Telling ripe food from spoiled food

• *Taking bra on and off* • • *Mending tears in clothing/sewing a button* • *Picking out the right sized clothing* • *Reading and understanding fabric labels* *Folding clothes and putting them away*		• *Setting the table*

Home Management Skills	Taking Care of Body/Health and Safety	Shopping/Community Outing Skills
- **Cleaning up toys, putting away in bin/basket** - **Washing a load of laundry in the washer and using the dryer** - **Sweeping the floor** - **Vacuuming the floor** - **Throwing away items in the trash** - **Taking out the trash**	- Taking medicine - Treating a wound - Knowing how to call 911 and what to say to the operator - Knowing how to stop bleeding from a cut - Knowing what to do in a fire - Knowing what to do in an emergency - Knowing own address	- Making a grocery/shopping list - Going to the grocery store - Finding food or items at the store - Purchasing food/items at the cash register at the store - Ordering items online to be shipped to home - Knowing how to check out at an online store - Using public transportation safely

- **Sorting out recyclables** - **Washing off countertops** - **Washing dishes** - **Loading dishwasher** - **Washing dishes by hand** - **Cleaning the shower/bathtub** - **Cleaning the**	- Knowing basic medical information about themselves - Understanding stranger safety - - Using an EpiPen for self or friends - Knowing how to call the doctor to make an appointment - Knowing how to go to the doctor - Knowing how to take over-the-counter medicine safely for common illnesses	- Walking around the neighborhood safely - Crossing a busy street and parking lot - Understanding car safety when driving - Knowing how to read road signs - Knowing how to go to a restaurant - Knowing how to go to the mall - Knowing how to go to the park Knowing how to go to the movie theater

toilet - *Putting away clothes* - *Putting dirty clothes in the hamper* - *Folding clothes* - *Making the bed* - *Sorting certain items in the home and organizing them into the correct location* - *Feeding Pets* - *Bringing in and putting away groceries*		

• Having basic home repair skills such as unclogging toilet or sink		

Functional Life Skills at School	Organization Skills	Money Skills
• Eating lunch in the lunchroom • Having an organized desk/locker • Getting the homework completed each day • Following school routine	• Getting up in time and getting ready for the day to go to school/work on time • Creating a checklist of things to do in the day • Identifying important tasks vs. nonimportant tasks	• Creating a budget • Knowing how to manage a checking account • Knowing how to manage a savings account • Knowing how to use an ATM • Knowing how to write a check

- **Hanging up backpack and coat** - **Getting ready for recess** - **Using the bathroom/rest room at school** - **Getting food from the vending machine** - **Navigating to the correct classroom** - **Staying at a school desk** - **Typing on a computer** - **Checking out a book from the library**	- *Meeting deadlines* - *Developing a daily routine* *Taking care of their things and knowing where they are in the house*	- Knowing how to pay with dollar bills - Knowing how to pay with debit/credit card - Understanding how credit works - Knowing how to save money - Knowing how to pay bills Understanding how taxes work

Get the Letter of Intent for Free

Building a relationship with our readers is the very best thing about writing. We occasionally send newsletters with details on new releases, special offers, and other bits of news relating to autism and special needs.

And if you sign up to the mailing list, we'll send you the Letter of Intent E-book, which is worth $35.00, for free. You can get Letter of Intent, for free, by signing up at https://diffnotless.com.

About the Letter of Intent E-book:

No one else knows your child as well as you do, and no one ever could. You are a walking encyclopedia of your child's history, experiences, habits, and wishes. If your child has special needs, the family's history adds a helpful chapter to your child's book, one detailing his unique medical, behavioral, and educational requirements.

A letter of intent helps your loved ones and your child manage a difficult transition when you no longer are the primary caregiver. A letter of intent is an important planning tool for parents of children with special needs (including adult children), and also guides your child's future caregivers in making the most appropriate life decisions for your child, including providing direction to your child's trustee in fulfilling his or her fiduciary responsibilities.

The letter of intent may be addressed to anyone you wish.

This document addresses the following points:

- emotional information,
- future vision for the child,
- biographical and personal information,
- medical information,
- personality traits and preferences,
- habits and hygiene,
- meals and dietary requirements, and
- much more.

Once you prepare, sign, and date the letter of intent, you should review the document annually and update it as necessary. It is important that you let your child's potential future caregiver know that the letter of intent exists and where it can be accessed; even better, you can review the document with the caregiver on an annual basis. The letter of intent should be placed with all of your other relevant legal and personal documents concerning your child.

Found This Book Useful? You Can Make a Big Difference

Reviews are the most powerful tools in our arsenal when it comes to getting attention for our books. Much as we'd like to, we don't have the financial muscle of a New York publisher. We can't take out full page ads in the newspaper or put posters on the subway.

But we do have something much more powerful and effective than that, and it's something that those publishers would kill to get their hands on.

A committed and loyal bunch of readers like you.

Honest reviews of our books help bring them to the attention of other readers.

If you've found this book useful, we would be very grateful if you could spend just five minutes leaving a review (it can be as short as you like) on the book's Amazon page.

Thank you very much.

Other Books by Susan Jules

Have you read them all?

What will happen to my Special Needs Child when I am gone: A Detailed Guide to Secure Your Child's Emotional and Financial Future— https://geni.us/At0afS

Let's Talk: A Conversational Skills Workbook for Children with Autism & Special Needs— https://geni.us/iwStb

105 Activities for Your Child With Autism and Special Needs: Enable them to Thrive, Interact, Develop and Play—https://geni.us/tSu9

Printed in Great Britain
by Amazon